McGraw-Hill's

500
European History
Questions

McGraw-Hill's

500

European History

Questions

Ace Your College Exams

Stephanie Muntone

New York Chicago San Francisco Lisbon London Madrid Mexico City
Milan New Delhi San Juan Seoul Singapore Sydney Toronto

1 2 3 4 5 6 7 8 9 10 11 12 13 14 15 16 17   QFR/QFR   1 9 8 7 6 5 4 3 2

ISBN   978-0-07-178035-3
MHID   0-07-178035-1

e-ISBN 978-0-07-178050-6
e-MHID 0-07-178050-5

Library of Congress Control Number 2011944608

McGraw-Hill products are available at special quantity discounts to use as premiums
and sales promotions or for use in corporate training programs. To contact a
representative, please e-mail us at bulksales@mcgraw-hill.com.

This book is printed on acid-free paper.

CONTENTS

INTRODUCTION

Congratulations! You've taken a big step toward achieving your best grade by purchasing *McGraw-Hill's 500 European History Questions*. We are here to help you improve your grades on classroom, midterm, and final exams. These 500 questions will help you study more effectively, use your preparation time wisely, and get the final grade you want.

This book gives you 500 multiple-choice questions that cover the most essential course material. Each question has a detailed answer explanation. These questions give you valuable independent practice to supplement your regular textbook and the groundwork you are already doing in the classroom.

You might be the kind of student who needs to study extra questions a few weeks before a big exam for a final review. Or you might be the kind of student who puts off preparing until right before a midterm or final. No matter what your preparation style, you will surely benefit from reviewing these 500 questions that closely parallel the content, format, and degree of difficulty of the questions found in typical college-level exams. These questions and their answer explanations are the ideal last-minute study tool for those final days before the test.

Remember the old saying "Practice makes perfect." If you practice with all the questions and answers in this book, we are certain that you will build the skills and confidence that are needed to ace your exams. Good luck!

—Editors of McGraw-Hill Education

CHAPTER 1

Europe Enters the Modern Era

The Italian Renaissance

1. The Black Death spread from
   (A) the Middle East to Europe
   (B) the Americas to Europe
   (C) Spain to South America
   (D) China to the Middle East
   (E) Europe to Africa

2. How did the Black Death help to bring about the Renaissance?
   (A) by causing massive westward migration
   (B) by stimulating trade between Asia and Europe
   (C) by weakening people's faith in medical science
   (D) by demonstrating that the Church was not all-powerful
   (E) by giving rise to a cultural exchange between East and West

3. What was the original purpose of the Council of Florence (1438)?
   (A) to discuss restoration and reconstruction of the Vatican
   (B) to translate the Bible into Western European languages
   (C) to reunite the Eastern Orthodox and Roman Catholic churches
   (D) to bring together scholars from many nations
   (E) to devise a plan to reform corrupt practices in the Church

4. Niccolò Machiavelli's *The Prince* (1513) was considered revolutionary because it suggested that above all else, a great ruler must be
   (A) pragmatic and realistic
   (B) ethical and moral
   (C) skilled in the use of arms
   (D) just and wise
   (E) intellectual and studious

5. Michelangelo Buonarroti made lasting contributions in all the following fields of endeavor EXCEPT
   (A) architecture
   (B) painting
   (C) philosophy
   (D) poetry
   (E) sculpture

6. Gutenberg's perfection of the process of printing with movable type can be described as the most important invention of the millennium because
   (A) it marked the end of the Church's domination of Western Europe
   (B) it led directly to the 16th-century Reformation
   (C) it enabled scholars to translate the Bible into modern European languages
   (D) it showed that Europeans could adapt and improve Asian technologies
   (E) it made literacy, and thus independent thought, possible for millions

7. What were the primary factors that caused scholars of the Renaissance to focus their studies more on Roman than Greek texts?
   (A) style and substance
   (B) the relative age of the manuscripts
   (C) language and location
   (D) religion and philosophy
   (E) political considerations

8. Which is NOT one reason why the European Renaissance began in Italy?
   (A) Italy was economically wealthy at the time.
   (B) The Italian city-states were politically stable.
   (C) Modern Italy was at the center of the ancient Roman Empire.
   (D) Italy was home to the greatest universities of Western Europe.
   (E) Many scholars gathered in Italy for the periodic Church councils.

9. Which of the following did NOT contribute to the loss of the Church's power and influence during the Renaissance?
   (A) the Church's inability to combat the Black Death
   (B) the rise in power of secular political figures such as Cesare Borgia
   (C) the revival of classical arts and ideas
   (D) the availability of printed books and the rise in individual literacy
   (E) the constant political warfare among the major European states

10. Which of the following was NOT one of the seven liberal arts studied by humanist scholars?
    (A) astronomy
    (B) geometry
    (C) logic
    (D) rhetoric
    (E) theology

11. Why did the powerful merchant princes of the Renaissance encourage their children to study the humanities, or liberal arts?
    (A) They wanted to spread liberal values throughout Italy and thence throughout Europe.
    (B) Liberal studies provided a good background for those wishing to enter the Church.
    (C) They wanted their children exposed to multiple points of view.
    (D) Liberal studies were good training for the professional world they would enter.
    (E) They wanted their children to be accepted in high society.

12. All of the following are notable artistic and/or literary figures of the Italian Renaissance EXCEPT
    (A) Henri Matisse in painting
    (B) Filippo Brunelleschi in architecture
    (C) Leonardo da Vinci in painting, drawing, and anatomy
    (D) Dante Alighieri in poetry and prose
    (E) Francesco Petrarch in poetry

13. Which best describes the government of Italy at the time of the Renaissance?
    (A) a number of independent city-states linked by a common language and culture
    (B) a unified nation ruled by an absolute hereditary monarch
    (C) a Catholic theocracy ruled by the pope
    (D) an empire centered in Rome and extending throughout the Mediterranean
    (E) a police state led by a military dictator

14. Which is NOT one way in which the wealthy merchant families of Italy gained enormous influence during the Renaissance?
    (A) They loaned money to the Church and therefore had some say in the Church's policy.
    (B) They commissioned architects and artists to create great masterpieces.
    (C) They sponsored international gatherings of scholars and theologians such as the Council of Florence.
    (D) They acquired political power and thus directed and controlled affairs of state.
    (E) They worked to lay the foundation for a unified nation of Italy that would come in the future.

The Reformation

15. Which of the following ruled Geneva as a virtual theocracy during the mid-1500s?
    (A) Jean Calvin
    (B) Desiderius Erasmus
    (C) John Knox
    (D) Martin Luther
    (E) Thomas More

16. Which best describes the original purpose of the Ninety-Five Theses?
    (A) to found a new Christian denomination that would rival Catholicism
    (B) to begin a public debate about certain practices of the Church
    (C) to provoke religious warfare between nations
    (D) to prove that the pope was not infallible
    (E) to destroy the Church's widespread influence throughout Europe

17. Who were the victims of the St. Bartholomew's Day Massacre in France?
    (A) Huguenots
    (B) Catholics
    (C) priests
    (D) common working people
    (E) the monarch and members of the royal court

18. What happened at the Diet of Worms in 1521?
- (A) The pope excommunicated Martin Luther.
- (B) Martin Luther published his Ninety-Five Theses.
- (C) Martin Luther refused to recant his statements about the Church.
- (D) The Holy Roman Emperor offered Martin Luther his personal protection.
- (E) The Holy Roman Emperor established Lutheranism as the religion of the empire.

19. The term *Protestant* first came into use to describe citizens who opposed official religious policy in
- (A) England
- (B) France
- (C) the Holy Roman Empire
- (D) Italy
- (E) Spain

20. The Peace of Augsburg (1555) was important because it established that
- (A) the pope did not have the authority to excommunicate a monarch from the Church
- (B) anyone accused of heresy would be tried by the Inquisition
- (C) Catholicism would continue to be the state religion of France
- (D) Presbyterianism would become the state religion of Scotland
- (E) each German prince had the right to determine the official religion of his own state

21. Predestination is the central doctrine of
- (A) Anglicanism
- (B) Calvinism
- (C) Eastern Orthodoxy
- (D) Lutheranism
- (E) Roman Catholicism

22. Predestination is defined as the belief that
- (A) worship services should be conducted in the language of the people
- (B) each individual believer must serve as his or her own priest
- (C) forms of secular enjoyment such as dancing and playing games are sinful
- (D) sincere repentance for one's sins earns the forgiveness of God
- (E) salvation is determined before birth and cannot be earned by faith or good works

23. What was the purpose of the Edict of Nantes?
    (A) to forbid Catholics to read any titles listed in the *Index of Forbidden Books*
    (B) to allow freedom of choice in religious worship throughout France
    (C) to declare that the monarch was the supreme head of the Church of England
    (D) to permit the electors of the Holy Roman Empire to name the official religions for their own states
    (E) to banish French Protestants, also called Huguenots, from France

24. Luther and his followers objected to the exchange of indulgences for financial donations to the Church on the grounds that
    (A) sinners should be punished even if they repented their sins
    (B) indulgences were being sold for such high prices that only rich people could buy them
    (C) indulgences were only intended to forgive sins committed by soldiers during the course of war
    (D) the Church had no power to promise immunity from punishment after death
    (E) the Church had no right to grant indulgences to believers

25. In which region of Europe did Protestantism spread most widely through the population?
    (A) on the Iberian Peninsula
    (B) throughout the Mediterranean
    (C) in central and northern Europe
    (D) in the Balkan region
    (E) in Eastern Europe

26. Henry IV of France espoused a policy allowing freedom of worship because
    (A) he was a devout Catholic
    (B) he was a famous theological scholar
    (C) he was more concerned with fighting foreign wars than with domestic policy
    (D) he hoped to wage war against Catholic Spain
    (E) he believed it would contribute to political stability

27. The term *Counter-Reformation* refers to which of the following?

(A) the hostility that developed between Lutherans and Calvinists

(B) the creation of rival sects of Calvinism, including Presbyterianism

(C) the Catholic Church's attempts to stamp out corruption in its own hierarchy

(D) widespread European protests against the granting of indulgences

(E) international debate over the Ninety-Five Theses

28. The Catholic Church attempted to restore its authority with the faithful in all these ways EXCEPT

(A) by convening the Council of Trent in 1545

(B) by electing popes and appointing cardinals who supported reform

(C) by publishing the *Index of Forbidden Books*

(D) by creating the Holy Office of the Inquisition

(E) by banning Protestantism in countries with Catholic monarchs

29. Catholic orders such as the Jesuits, the Ursulines, and the Capucines were founded with all the following purposes EXCEPT

(A) to educate children and youths throughout Europe

(B) to preach against ordinary fun (such as dancing or playing card games)

(C) to set an example of piety, chastity, and humility for the faithful

(D) to serve and help the poor in all parts of the world

(E) to persuade those they helped to convert to Catholicism

30. What was the basic purpose of the Roman Inquisition?

(A) to try people who were accused of heresy

(B) to extract confessions by means of torture and terror

(C) to turn accused heretics over to the civil authorities for trial and punishment

(D) to convert Protestants to Catholicism

(E) to conduct public executions of convicted heretics

CHAPTER 2

Absolute Monarchy in Early Modern Europe

The Rise of the Russian Empire to 1613

31. What is the main reason why no prosperous mercantile middle class developed in medieval Russia?

(A) The Russian monarchy and aristocracy did not want a middle class to develop.

(B) The Russian government was too politically conservative to invest in the economy.

(C) The Russian climate and topography prevented easy, frequent travel within the empire.

(D) Russian artisans were not as skilled as their Western European counterparts.

(E) The Russians were Eastern Orthodox Catholics.

32. Why was Ivan IV able to remain in power despite his mental instability?

(A) He remained personally popular and beloved among the common people.

(B) The Orthodox clergy remained loyal to him as the head of the state.

(C) There was no legal or constitutional procedure to remove an incapable ruler.

(D) There were no rival claimants to the throne who were any better qualified than Ivan.

(E) Ivan was the last of his family, so he had no legitimate heirs to succeed him.

33. Russia truly began its history as a modern nation-state when

(A) Dmitri of the Don led the Russians to victory over the Tatars in the Battle of Kulikovo

(B) Ivan III married the Byzantine princess Zoe Palaeologos

(C) Ivan III withheld the customary annual tribute to the Tatars, forcing their withdrawal from Russia

(D) Ivan IV created the *Oprichnina* and made it responsible only to himself

(E) Vasili II decreed that only his direct descendants could inherit the Russian throne

34. In early modern Russia, why was there no strong legislative body to balance the power of the czar?

(A) The czar did not trust the boyars to be loyal to the throne.

(B) The Eastern Orthodox faith was not compatible with a balance of power in the government.

(C) The boyars' estates were too far from Moscow to permit frequent travel.

(D) The Russian people were loyal to the czar and did not want a strong legislature.

(E) The czar was more interested in military victories than in administration.

35. The "Time of Troubles" that lasted from about 1590 to 1613 was characterized by all of the following EXCEPT

(A) peasant uprisings

(B) competition for the throne

(C) war with foreign kingdoms

(D) widespread crop failure and famine

(E) wholesale executions of dissenters

36. Which best accounts for the conquering mentality of the rulers of Muscovy during the late Middle Ages?

(A) the fact that Moscow was considered "the Third Rome"

(B) the fact that the rulers of Muscovy had little contact with any Western rulers

(C) the fact that Moscow was the empire's capital city

(D) the fact that Muscovy had a mild climate

(E) the fact that Muscovy had no natural, geographical defenses

37. The major goals of the Russian princes and czars from the 14th through the 16th centuries included all of the following EXCEPT

(A) to put an end to Tatar authority in the region once and for all
(B) to enter into an era of cultural and intellectual exchange with Western Europe
(C) to expand Russia's borders for strategic and trade purposes
(D) to establish an absolute Russian monarchy in a central capital city
(E) to achieve royal control over all ranks and elements of Russian society

38. How did Poland hope to capitalize on Russia's Time of Troubles?

(A) by converting the Russian population to Roman Catholicism
(B) by establishing formal diplomatic relations with Russia
(C) by aiding the Russian people in a planned uprising against Moscow
(D) by taking over Russian territory and thus expanding its own borders
(E) by conquering Russia and making it part of a Polish empire

39. Boris Godunov was an unpopular ruler primarily because

(A) he had been elected to the throne rather than inheriting it directly
(B) his weak, indecisive personality made him unfit to rule
(C) he refused to consult the boyars on matters of national policy
(D) he was the brother-in-law of Czar Feodor
(E) he had served in the *Oprichnina* under Ivan IV

40. Why did Boris Godunov issue the *ukase* (royal edict) of 1597?

(A) to put down a rebellion that broke out among the armed forces
(B) to restrict the peasants' right to move about freely through the realm
(C) to streamline the civil service and make it more efficient
(D) to levy new taxes on the common people
(E) to ensure that his children would inherit the Russian throne

41. Why did so many Russian noblemen join the military during the 15th century?

(A) because military service was rewarded with large land grants
(B) because they were eager to defeat the Tatars
(C) because they believed the privileged class owed this duty to the state
(D) to obey new laws that required them to serve
(E) to show their personal loyalty to the throne

42. What was the most notable result of contact with Western Europe under Ivan III?

(A) The Russian army was enlarged and reorganized.

(B) The Eastern Orthodox Church was reunited with the Roman Catholic Church.

(C) Russian citizens began to have a greater voice in their own government.

(D) Russia acquired its first written constitution.

(E) The Kremlin was redesigned and rebuilt.

43. Which is the most likely reason for Ivan IV's swift fall after the highly successful first half of his reign?

(A) repeated Russian losses on the battlefield

(B) a conspiracy among rival claimants to the throne

(C) a conspiracy among the boyars to strengthen their own powers

(D) the serious threat of a popular uprising

(E) his own mental instability and physical illness

44. The system of government in early modern Russia made which of the following the most important factor in the stability of the empire?

(A) the strength and size of the military

(B) the relations between the monarch and the Orthodox Church

(C) the monarch's personality and leadership ability

(D) the success or failure of the annual harvest

(E) the efficiency of the bureaucracy

45. The *Oprichnina*, created by Ivan IV, is best described as

(A) a secret state police force

(B) a religious brotherhood

(C) a military company responsible to guard the Kremlin

(D) a rogue militia reporting directly to the czar

(E) a pro forma legislature that existed only to carry out the czar's wishes

Spain and the Holy Roman Empire in the 16th and 17th Centuries

46. Why did Isabel and Ferdinand establish the Spanish Inquisition?

(A) to enable them to banish all Protestants from their kingdom

(B) to force all the people to observe the same religious faith

(C) to achieve absolute control over the aristocracy

(D) to convince the pope in Rome of their personal loyalty

(E) to hold major ceremonial events for the mass of the people

47. As a result of the defeat of the Spanish Armada,

(A) Spain ceded its North American colonies to England

(B) the North African Muslims were driven out of the Iberian Peninsula

(C) the Holy Roman Empire severed its alliance with Spain

(D) Spain ceased to be a dominant European power

(E) Ferdinand of Aragon and Isabel of Castile married, thus creating a united Spanish monarchy

48. Which is NOT one reason for conflict between England and Spain during the late 1500s?

(A) Elizabeth I's resentment over Philip II's treatment of Queen Mary during the latter's lifetime

(B) competition for colonies in the Western Hemisphere

(C) English piracy against Spanish ships

(D) patterns of foreign alliances

(E) religious differences

49. What was the root cause of the strong, lasting alliance between Spain and the Holy Roman Empire?

(A) They shared a common geographical border.

(B) Their monarchs were members of the same immediate family.

(C) They worked together to expel the North African Muslims from Spain.

(D) They defied the pope by establishing their own state religions.

(E) They were both longtime enemies of France.

50. During the pre-industrial era, which of the following exports became the mainstay of the Spanish economy?

(A) wool
(B) vinegar
(C) fine wines, port, and sherry
(D) olives and olive oil
(E) wheat

51. Which best explains the principle of the divine right of kings, by which Isabel and Ferdinand ruled Spain?

(A) The monarch is both a literal and a figurative descendant of God.
(B) The Church and the monarch work together to maintain a stable and homogeneous realm.
(C) God's wisdom placed the monarch in his or her position of authority; therefore the monarch's authority cannot be challenged or questioned.
(D) The monarch has the absolute right to rule because the monarch and the people share the same faith.
(E) The monarch is considered God's representative on earth.

52. The term *Reconquista* refers to which of the following?

(A) the marriage of Isabel and Ferdinand
(B) the ouster of the Muslims from the Iberian Peninsula
(C) the expansion of the Spanish Empire into South America
(D) the Spanish participation in the African slave trade
(E) the Spanish takeover of various Italian provinces

53. During the mid-1500s, Holy Roman Emperor Ferdinand I faced a constant threat of invasion from

(A) Austria
(B) France
(C) Italy
(D) Poland
(E) Turkey

54. Which best describes the religious policy of Ferdinand I, as both Holy Roman Emperor and king of Hungary and Bohemia?

(A) He banned the practice of Catholicism within the realm.
(B) He banned the practice of Protestantism within the realm.
(C) He encouraged Catholicism but permitted freedom of worship in the realm.
(D) He denied any papal authority within the realm.
(E) He thoroughly reorganized the Church hierarchy within the realm.

55. Which best describes the Holy Roman Empire in the period before the Thirty Years' War?

(A) an association of kingdoms with independent rulers all under the authority of one emperor

(B) a constitutional monarchy with a strong parliament of electors

(C) an autocracy under the absolute rule of a single monarch

(D) a confederation of independent kingdoms united for financial and security concerns

(E) a monarchy with a freely elected senate, run by an efficient and far-reaching bureaucracy

56. As Queen of Castile in her own right, why did Isabel share some of her authority with Ferdinand?

(A) She had no experience of governing and therefore could not rule effectively on her own.

(B) She preferred a dual monarchy to sharing her authority with a parliament.

(C) She had religious scruples about ruling a kingdom because she was a woman.

(D) She was mentally unstable and unfit to rule on her own.

(E) She was concerned that the people would not accept an absolute female monarch.

57. In 1555, Philip II inherited a kingdom of Spain that was characterized by all of the following EXCEPT

(A) a prosperous economy

(B) religious tolerance

(C) a strong navy

(D) a contented aristocracy

(E) a vast colonial empire

58. Ferdinand I laid the foundation for a unified Austrian state by taking all these steps EXCEPT

(A) making German the official language of the empire

(B) dividing his government into executive, administrative, and judicial departments

(C) making the wealthy landowners responsible for day-to-day provincial government

(D) reorganizing and streamlining the civil service

(E) tolerating freedom of choice in religious worship

59. Which is NOT one reason why Spain developed into a highly conservative monarchy?

(A) The ruling Hapsburg family was devoutly Catholic.

(B) The monarchy insisted on ruling a religiously homogeneous nation.

(C) The hereditary nobles were given so many privileges that they did not agitate for greater political power.

(D) The Inquisition used fear to keep the people from rising up against the authorities.

(E) The economy was stagnant and largely dependent on taxing the people beyond their means.

60. During the 15th and 16th centuries, Spain formed alliances with numerous European states by means of

(A) royal marriages

(B) political treaties

(C) military conquest

(D) colonization

(E) imperialism

Tudor and Early Stuart England

61. The reign of Queen Mary I is best remembered for

(A) her romantic marriage to Philip II of Spain

(B) her sponsorship of artists and men of letters

(C) her judicial persecution and execution of hundreds of Protestants

(D) her establishment of charity schools for children of the poor

(E) her insistence on ruling without advice or interference from Parliament

62. Which best describes King James I's view of the British Parliament?

(A) It should exist only to carry out the king's wishes.

(B) It should advise the king only on matters of foreign policy.

(C) It should function as a powerful lawmaking body.

(D) It should play an important role in the administration of justice.

(E) It should serve as a legislative model for other nations to copy.

63. The Anglican Church, or Church of England, was formally created in 1534 when

(A) Henry VIII divorced Catherine of Aragon
(B) Henry VIII married Anne Boleyn
(C) Pope Paul III excommunicated Henry VIII
(D) Thomas Cranmer was appointed archbishop of Canterbury
(E) Parliament passed the Act of Supremacy

64. Why did Elizabeth I court the love and personal loyalty of all her subjects?

(A) to make them more likely to vote for her
(B) to guard against the possibility of assassination or a palace coup
(C) to make them forget that she had no right to the throne
(D) to keep them interested in the question of her possible marriage to a foreign monarch
(E) to gain their support for her anti-Catholic policies

65. Which best sums up Elizabeth I's main goal as monarch of England?

(A) to shift the balance of power in government from the legislature to the monarch
(B) to see England become the dominant power in Europe
(C) to expand the British Empire by acquiring colonies overseas
(D) to win a series of religious wars
(E) to rule a peaceful and prosperous kingdom

66. All of the following are among the great literary or artistic achievements of the English Renaissance EXCEPT

(A) the King James Bible
(B) the plays of William Shakespeare
(C) the portraits of Hans Holbein
(D) the operas of Benjamin Britten
(E) the lyric poems of John Donne

67. Why did King Henry VIII abandon the Church in the 1530s?

(A) so that he could remarry and beget a male heir
(B) for personal reasons of religious faith
(C) because he wanted church services conducted in English
(D) as an act of political defiance against an enemy nation
(E) because most British subjects were anti-Catholic

68. Which did NOT contribute to the English defeat of the Spanish Armada?

(A) Allies came to the defense of England but not of Spain.

(B) Major storms blew up at sea at an ideal time for the British side.

(C) The British ships were lighter and faster.

(D) The British used superior strategy.

(E) The Spaniards were too far from their sources of supply.

69. The Thirty-Nine Articles, ratified under Elizabeth I in 1563, are best described as

(A) the civil rights of the British people

(B) the major tenets of the Church of England

(C) provisions of the treaty England made with Spain after the Armada

(D) the English civil and criminal law code

(E) rules for debate and the passage of bills in Parliament

70. Why did Elizabeth I order the execution of her cousin Mary Queen of Scots in 1587?

(A) Mary provoked the Scots into an all-out war with England.

(B) Mary refused to agree to a dual monarchy of England and Scotland.

(C) Mary was a Catholic in an Anglican realm.

(D) Mary participated in a plot to assassinate Elizabeth.

(E) Mary was the rightful heir to the English throne.

71. *The Book of Common Prayer*, originally published in 1549, is historically significant because

(A) it was a magnificent English translation of the Hebrew and Greek testaments

(B) it set forth the religious rites of the Anglican Church in English

(C) it was the first European book printed with movable metal type

(D) it described the lives and persecutions of Protestants executed for their faith

(E) it listed nearly a hundred theological propositions for debate

72. How did Queen Elizabeth's unmarried status affect England's foreign policy during her reign?
    (A) She was free to bestow rich rewards on servants of the crown such as Sir Walter Raleigh.
    (B) It made it expedient for her to allow her chief ministers an extraordinary amount of authority.
    (C) Any monarch considering marriage to her would have to maintain good relations with England.
    (D) England had to appear militarily powerful because other nations would assume a nation ruled by a woman was weak.
    (E) It made it possible for England to begin to build a vast colonial empire.

73. Which is NOT one serious issue that confronted James I during his reign?
    (A) discontentment among the religious minorities within England
    (B) clashes between Protestants and Catholics in Ireland
    (C) the neglected condition of the royal navy
    (D) parliamentary desire for more influence over matters of state
    (E) loud and persistent calls for self-determination from Scotland

74. What was James I's solution to his disagreements with Parliament?
    (A) He dissolved Parliament and governed without it for 10 years.
    (B) He agreed to consult Parliament more regularly on matters of policy.
    (C) He consulted his chief ministers about how best to resolve the dispute.
    (D) He took his case to the people by publishing a pamphlet outlining his position on Parliament's role.
    (E) He abdicated the throne when he realized he could not govern without giving way to parliamentary demands.

75. Which of the following best explains England's relative lack of involvement in European wars and other conflicts under the Tudors and James I?
    (A) economic depression
    (B) geographical isolation
    (C) religious tolerance
    (D) military weakness
    (E) colonial ambition

hirty Years' War

76. Which of these events touched off the Thirty Years' War in 1618?
    (A) the Defenestration of Prague
    (B) the election of Ferdinand II as Holy Roman Emperor
    (C) the publication of the Letter of Majesty
    (D) the passage of the Edict of Restitution
    (E) the installation of Frederich Wittelsbach as King of Bohemia

77. Which best explains why France dreaded a possible alliance between Spain and a united German nation?
    (A) Spain and the future Germany would both be strong Catholic nations.
    (B) France was geographically between Spain and the future Germany.
    (C) Such an alliance would force France to come to terms with England.
    (D) Such an alliance would create a balance of power in Europe.
    (E) Such an alliance would destroy the balance of power in Europe.

78. Which statement does NOT describe Sweden's involvement in the Thirty Years' War?
    (A) It entered the war in order to aid its Protestant allies within the Holy Roman Empire.
    (B) It hoped to gain valuable territory on the Baltic Sea and thus take control of major trade routes.
    (C) It accepted financial and military aid from France.
    (D) It had some of the era's best military leaders and won a number of crucial battles.
    (E) It withdrew from the war and from the world stage when King Gustav II Adolph was killed in battle.

79. Which of the following best explains why the prospects of German unification were very dim in 1648?
    (A) The Holy Roman Empire was no longer allied with Spain.
    (B) Leaders of the Protestant German states could not reconcile the hostility between their Calvinist and Lutheran subjects.
    (C) The German states had suffered tremendous losses during the war.
    (D) The emperor refused to consider establishing religious freedom within the Holy Roman Empire.
    (E) Both France and Spain wanted to keep the German states from forming a strong official union.

80. The Thirty Years' War can be accurately described as any of the following EXCEPT
    (A) a conflict over religion
    (B) a dynastic quarrel between powerful families
    (C) a power struggle among nations
    (D) a popular uprising in the name of greater political freedom
    (E) a grab for strategically and/or economically desirable territory

81. What was the source of the spark that began the Thirty Years' War?
    (A) rival claims to the throne of Bohemia
    (B) tension between the Lutheran aristocracy and the Catholic bureaucracy
    (C) an armed invasion from Sweden
    (D) a series of new laws revoking the privileges and rights of Protestants
    (E) a declaration of French support for the Protestant side in the war

82. What was France's main motive for entering the Thirty Years' War?
    (A) to come to the aid of a fellow Catholic nation
    (B) to cement an alliance with the rising nation-state of Russia
    (C) to undermine the power and position of the Holy Roman Empire
    (D) to expand its own territorial borders
    (E) to prevent a possible alliance between Spain and the Holy Roman Empire

83. Which nation briefly became a major European power during the Thirty Years' War?
    (A) Belgium
    (B) England
    (C) France
    (D) Spain
    (E) Sweden

84. The Peace of Westphalia signed at the end of the Thirty Years' War contained all these provisions EXCEPT
    (A) it decreed that no Catholic could be chosen Holy Roman Emperor
    (B) it gave valuable territories to France and Sweden
    (C) it created a unified Austrian empire
    (D) it made Prussia an independent state within the Holy Roman Empire
    (E) it overturned a ban on Protestantism within the Holy Roman Empire

85. Which nation emerged from the Thirty Years' War as the dominant European power?

(A) Austria
(B) England
(C) France
(D) the Holy Roman Empire
(E) Spain

86. The Peace of Westphalia marked the first time in European history that national leaders agreed together on

(A) religious tolerance
(B) maintaining a balance of power
(C) the creation of an international peacekeeping organization
(D) the payment of reparations by the aggressor nation
(E) an international war-crimes tribunal

87. The Thirty Years' War saw the deployment of all these military innovations, gradually arrived at over the course of the 16th century, EXCEPT

(A) the use of bronze artillery (cannon)
(B) the increased reliance on infantry
(C) the increased mobility of the armies
(D) the development of cast-iron guns
(E) the deployment of greater numbers of soldiers

88. When Ferdinand became king of Bohemia and revoked the Letter of Majesty, he provoked a violent uprising led by

(A) the students, artists, and intellectuals
(B) the Lutheran landed gentry
(C) the Catholic bureaucracy
(D) the elected legislature
(E) the common people

89. Spain was unable to aid its allies in the Holy Roman Empire for all these reasons EXCEPT

(A) Spanish troops were fully occupied in fighting the French
(B) the Spanish army was too far from its sources of supply
(C) Spain had sent the bulk of its troops to the Americas
(D) the Spanish government was distracted by uprisings at home
(E) Spain had never recovered financially or militarily from the defeat of the Armada

90. Which best describes the Hapsburg territory after the end of the war in 1648?

    (A) largely Catholic
    (B) largely Lutheran
    (C) largely Calvinist
    (D) religiously diverse
    (E) religiously tolerant

England from Charles I to the Glorious Revolution

91. What was the purpose of the Petition of Right of 1628?

    (A) to forbid taxation without the consent of Parliament
    (B) to dissolve Parliament until it agreed to the monarch's demands for obedience
    (C) to set forth the individual rights of the British people
    (D) to alter the system of parliamentary elections
    (E) to request the monarch to end discrimination against non-Anglican citizens

92. *Puritans* is the term most often used to identify which of the following English religious groups?

    (A) Roman Catholics
    (B) Calvinists or Presbyterians
    (C) low-church Anglicans
    (D) high-church Anglicans
    (E) Methodists

93. During the 16th century, the balance of power in the English government shifted in favor of

    (A) the monarch
    (B) the legislature
    (C) the aristocracy
    (D) the common people
    (E) the military

94. Over which of the following issues did Scots troops invade England in 1640?

(A) opposition to the imposition of Anglican religious rites on the Church of Scotland

(B) support for an official union of the two kingdoms

(C) opposition to taxes that had been assessed without parliamentary consent

(D) support for the English Parliament in its conflict with the monarchy

(E) opposition to the monarch's foreign policy

95. England under the rule of Oliver Cromwell is best described as

(A) a constitutional monarchy

(B) an absolute monarchy

(C) a democratic republic

(D) a military dictatorship

(E) a popular democracy

96. Which of the following led directly to the passage of the English Bill of Rights?

(A) the Glorious Revolution

(B) the English Civil War

(C) the failure of the Exclusion Bill

(D) the formation of the Whig and Tory parties

(E) the Restoration

97. Charles I was generally unpopular for all these reasons EXCEPT

(A) he was stiff and awkward in his dealings with people

(B) he was eager to expand England's colonial empire in North America

(C) he did not believe in consulting Parliament on national policy

(D) he was married to a French Catholic princess

(E) his religious beliefs were rigidly high-Anglican

98. Oliver Cromwell's administration featured all of the following EXCEPT

(A) relative religious tolerance toward all groups except Catholics

(B) the closing of all theaters, saloons, and gambling houses

(C) good relations with Parliament

(D) persecution of the Catholic Irish

(E) censorship of the press

99. What was the purpose of the Exclusion Bill, introduced in Parliament in 1679 under Charles II?

(A) to grant the citizens certain fundamental civil rights
(B) to set forth the specific powers of Parliament
(C) to codify the monarch's role in the British government
(D) to unite Scotland and England officially as the United Kingdom
(E) to bar the king's brother and heir from inheriting the throne

100. What was the direct cause of the English Civil War that began in 1642?

(A) Parliament's demand that it be summoned at least once every three years
(B) a major uprising of the Irish Catholic nobility against the Protestant colonizers of Ireland
(C) religious disputes between the king and the leading members of Parliament
(D) Parliament's passage of a series of laws without the king's consent
(E) the king's establishment of special law courts without parliamentary consent

101. The term *Glorious Revolution* refers to which of the following?

(A) the ratification of the British constitution
(B) the flight of James II and the coronation of William and Mary
(C) the rise to power of Oliver Cromwell
(D) the ratification of the English Bill of Rights
(E) the execution of King Charles I

102. All of the following historically significant events occurred during the reign of Charles II EXCEPT

(A) an unsuccessful armed rebellion against the crown
(B) the founding of the Royal Society
(C) a major outbreak of the bubonic plague
(D) the construction of St. Paul's Cathedral
(E) the Great Fire that destroyed ancient central London

103. The Declaration of Indulgence, granted by James II in 1687 and 1688, granted

(A) freedom from persecution to all Catholics in the realm
(B) absolute freedom of choice in religious worship to all British citizens
(C) the return of property that the Catholic Church had been forced to surrender to the crown under Henry VIII
(D) political asylum to Catholics who had fled England under Cromwell
(E) pardons to those who had been imprisoned for their religious beliefs at any time since 1603

104. All of the following motives persuaded citizens to side with the Cavaliers rather than the Roundheads during the Civil War EXCEPT

(A) belief that turning against a legitimate monarch was treason
(B) fear that the triumph of Puritanism would bring anarchy to the nation
(C) genuine support for the Church of England
(D) fear for the loss of their personal fortunes if the Roundheads won the war
(E) outrage over Parliament's declared intention to execute the king

105. The coronation and reign of Charles II are generally referred to as

(A) the Interregnum
(B) the Restoration
(C) the Glorious Revolution
(D) the Carolingian era
(E) the Regency

France Under Louis XIII and Louis XIV

106. During the reign of Louis XIV, the Estates General

(A) always agreed to the king's demands
(B) held no sessions at all
(C) met only under extraordinary circumstances
(D) organized vigorous opposition to the king's foreign policy
(E) attempted to pass a program of social reform

107. Why did Louis XIV require the titled aristocrats to spend part of each year at Versailles?

    (A) to aid him in crushing popular uprisings
    (B) to advise him on matters of national policy
    (C) to stimulate the French economy by requiring lavish spending
    (D) to weaken the bonds between them and their tenants and estates
    (E) to prevent them from conspiring against him

108. Which of the following was the chief cause of the series of rebellions collectively known as the Fronde?

    (A) new taxes
    (B) widespread famine
    (C) enforced military service
    (D) restrictions on freedom of movement
    (E) censorship of the press

109. During the War of Spanish Succession, European nations united to prevent the creation of a close alliance or formal union between

    (A) England and Belgium
    (B) Belgium and France
    (C) France and Spain
    (D) Spain and Austria
    (E) Austria and England

110. Louis XIV unintentionally helped to bring about the Enlightenment by

    (A) calling for a variety of public-works projects that provided jobs for the unemployed
    (B) publicly expressing his disbelief in a number of basic Catholic doctrines
    (C) allowing the Estates General full participation in the government as a lawmaking body
    (D) passing a series of laws that established freedom of religious worship
    (E) sponsoring the creation of the royal academies of art, science, and letters

111. The Peace of Alès of 1629 called for or resulted in all of the following EXCEPT

    (A) overturning the Edict of Nantes of 1598

    (B) ending the siege of La Rochelle

    (C) reaffirming the policy of religious tolerance established by Henry IV

    (D) revoking certain self-governing privileges of La Rochelle and Montauban

    (E) neutralizing the military and political threat caused by the Huguenot presence in the region

112. In the late 17th century, Huguenots experienced all the following forms of persecution EXCEPT

    (A) the physical destruction of hundreds of their church buildings

    (B) wholesale enforced banishment from France

    (C) a ban on national meetings of religious leaders

    (D) restrictions on eligibility for certain professions and guilds

    (E) assessments of supplementary taxes

113. The "Cardinal Ministers" Richelieu and Mazarin oversaw all these changes to the political structure of France EXCEPT

    (A) enlarging the army to about five times the size it had been before the Thirty Years' War

    (B) filling official positions at court based on merit rather than birth

    (C) enlarging the powers of the *intendants* to oversee provincial government

    (D) streamlining and facilitating the collection of taxes

    (E) helping to create a legislature with real lawmaking powers

114. Foreign wars conducted during the reign of Louis XIV from 1667 to 1713 resulted in all the following setbacks and losses EXCEPT

    (A) losing North American colonies to Britain in 1713

    (B) failing to unite the crowns of Spain and France

    (C) backing the losing Stuart dynasty in Britain

    (D) failing in the royal policy of "reunion" (annexing certain territories with ties to France)

    (E) neglecting the French navy to build up the army

115. All of the following helped to sustain France economically during the 17th century, despite extravagant royal spending, EXCEPT

(A) the construction of the Canal du Midi, which linked the Mediterranean Sea and the Atlantic Ocean

(B) the building of massive fortifications on France's northern and eastern borders

(C) government support for luxury industries such as glass-blowing and tapestry-weaving

(D) trading with French colonies in North America and the Caribbean on favorable terms

(E) the adoption of protective tariffs

116. Which of the following was NOT among the significant literary figures of 17th-century France?

(A) Jean de la Fontaine

(B) Victor Hugo

(C) Molière

(D) Jean Racine

(E) Madame de Sévigné

117. War broke out between France and the Netherlands in the late 1600s over the issue of

(A) religion

(B) territory

(C) economics

(D) colonial expansion

(E) popular insurrection

118. Jean-Baptiste Colbert is a significant figure in French history in the field of

(A) economics and finance

(B) arms and the military

(C) science

(D) the arts

(E) foreign policy

119. Louis XIV demonstrated royal support for the arts and sciences in all the following ways EXCEPT

(A) establishing royal academies in several disciplines
(B) insisting on a measure of royal censorship of the arts and letters
(C) sponsoring a number of monumental building projects in Paris and elsewhere
(D) providing numerous artists and writers with annual incomes
(E) encouraging talented foreign artists and artisans to work in France

120. Which does NOT describe an important aspect of the lives of French aristocrats in the 17th and 18th centuries?

(A) They were given many privileges in order to ensure their continued support for the monarchy.
(B) They generally lived on credit rather than paying their debts.
(C) Attending the king at Versailles forced them into major expense and debt.
(D) They were more and more alienated from the peasants and tenants on their estates.
(E) Male aristocrats were required to serve a certain term in the military, usually in high-ranking positions.

The Great Powers of Eastern Europe: Austria, Russia, and Prussia to 1815

121. Joseph II of Austria instituted all the following major social reforms EXCEPT

(A) the relaxation of censorship of the press
(B) the expansion of civil rights of non-Catholics
(C) the nationalization of major industries
(D) the administrative reorganization of the Catholic Church
(E) the founding of a system of free public education

122. All of these composers were significant figures in the musical world of Vienna during the classical era (late 1700s into early 1800s) EXCEPT

(A) Ludwig van Beethoven
(B) Christoph Willibald Gluck
(C) Franz Joseph Haydn
(D) Wolfgang Amadeus Mozart
(E) Richard Strauss

123. What was the purpose of the Pragmatic Sanction?
  (A) to transfer certain territories from Austria to Prussia
  (B) to make daughters, as well as sons, eligible to inherit the Austrian throne
  (C) to establish a joint monarchy of Prussia and Austria
  (D) to prevent the creation of a unified German nation
  (E) to take over strategically important territory from Poland

124. Frederick the Great of Prussia accomplished all of the following during his reign EXCEPT
  (A) sending troops into Silesia and wresting it from the Austrian Empire
  (B) making the civil service more effective by insisting on merit-based advancement
  (C) developing the army into the most feared and mighty military force in Europe
  (D) making Prussia the dominant nation-state in Europe
  (E) leading Prussia to victory over France in the Seven Years' War

125. Peter the Great established St. Petersburg as Russia's new capital city in order to
  (A) protect Russia from potential invasion by a Western European power
  (B) symbolize his belief that Russia was culturally a Western European nation
  (C) facilitate foreign trade with Western Europe
  (D) command the attendance and service of the aristocracy
  (E) prove to his subjects that he ruled Russia by divine right

126. Which of the following kingdoms quickly became especially respected and feared throughout Europe for its military might?
  (A) Austria
  (B) Bohemia
  (C) Hungary
  (D) Poland
  (E) Prussia

127. Joseph II's program of social reform was highly unpopular with which of the following?
  (A) the wealthy merchants
  (B) the artisans
  (C) the students and intellectuals
  (D) the liberals
  (E) the conservatives

128. The reign of Catherine the Great of Russia oversaw all the following EXCEPT

(A) the reunion of the Old Believers with the mainstream Eastern Orthodox Church

(B) the securing of Russian access to the Black Sea and the Dardanelles Strait

(C) the social elevation of the nobility in exchange for their virtual abandonment of political influence

(D) reorganization of the provincial governments in response to a major peasant rebellion

(E) support for the arts and sciences and higher education, including women's education

129. Prussia's 1772 acquisition of Polish territory on the Baltic, which it named West Prussia, was important because

(A) it enlarged Prussia to nearly twice its previous size

(B) it gave Prussia a geographical base from which to attack Sweden

(C) it provided Prussia with access to the Baltic Sea

(D) the new land was rich in natural resources that Prussia lacked

(E) it made the kingdom of Prussia into one contiguous land mass

130. From 1640 through the 18th century, the ruling Hohenzollern family took all the following steps to make Prussia a modern nation-state EXCEPT

(A) building up the army in size, strength, and expertise

(B) pacifying the nobility by giving its most able men responsible government posts

(C) making the civil service increasingly more efficient

(D) uniting all territories inherited by the family under the king's control

(E) establishing a strong legislature and working together to write a national constitution

131. Which was NOT a factor in the Swedish defeat in the Great Northern War fought against Russia the early 1700s?

(A) The Russians outnumbered the Swedes.

(B) Peter the Great was a better military commander than Charles XII of Sweden.

(C) The Russian scorched-earth policy prevented the Swedish troops from foraging.

(D) The Swedes had only a few cannon while the Russians had dozens.

(E) Thousands of Swedish troops succumbed to the bitter Russian winter.

132. When the ruling Hohenzollern family first determined to make Prussia into a modern nation-state, they faced all the following obstacles EXCEPT

(A) a vulnerable geographic location—central and with no natural defenses

(B) weak and ineffective leadership

(C) a small amount of contiguous territory

(D) almost no natural resources

(E) a small population

133. Which was NOT one result or aspect of the Ottoman Turkish attack on Vienna in 1682–1683?

(A) Most of the European nation-states set aside their differences to support Austria.

(B) The Ottoman Empire entered a long era of decline.

(C) Austria and Prussia forged a lasting alliance against the Turks.

(D) The era of Turkish attempts to expand into central Europe was permanently ended.

(E) The Austrian Empire was able to attempt serious expansion to the east and south.

134. A major popular uprising in Russia in 1648 had all these results EXCEPT

(A) serfdom was formally established

(B) a new law code was published

(C) the nobility gained strength and power

(D) the czar agreed to share some governing powers with the legislature

(E) certain tax reforms were passed

135. Joseph II of Austria is best described as

(A) a benevolent autocrat who believed he was the best judge of what was good for his subjects

(B) an absolute dictator who literally believed in the divine right of kings

(C) a warrior-king who repeatedly led his troops to victory in battle

(D) a constitutional monarch who ruled in cooperation with the legislative assembly

(E) a figurehead who appeared on state and ceremonial occasions but who had no political power

136. All of the following developments in the late 1700s helped to pave the way for the eventual unification of Germany EXCEPT

(A) the growth of a highly educated elite
(B) a shift toward merit rather than birth as the basis for professional advancement
(C) the gradual standardization of the spoken and written German language
(D) the increase of political awareness and participation by the lower classes
(E) the increase of the bureaucracy

137. Which best describes the status of Poland from 1795 to 1918?

(A) It was a Russian protectorate.
(B) It was occupied by Sweden.
(C) It was entirely taken over by Austria, Prussia, and Russia.
(D) It was a puppet kingdom under Prussian and Russian sway.
(E) It was a weak but independent absolute monarchy.

138. Czar Feodor oversaw all the following reforms to the Russian government EXCEPT

(A) the change from a land-based to a household-based tax system
(B) the reorganization and enlargement of the standing army
(C) the abolition of the system of precedence that tied civil-service rank to birth
(D) the streamlining of the bureaucracy in Moscow
(E) the elimination of the Streltsy

139. What was Prussia's major goal in the Seven Years' War?

(A) to gain supremacy over the British and French navies
(B) to reclaim strategically important Austrian territory from France
(C) to retain valuable Austrian territory it had seized in the 1740s
(D) to acquire territory in North America
(E) to unite the kingdoms of Austria and Prussia into one great German power

140. Sweden, Russia, and France banded together during the Seven Years' War with the main objective of crushing

(A) Britain
(B) Prussia
(C) Spain
(D) Italy
(E) Austria

141. Peter the Great was determined to westernize Russia for all these reasons EXCEPT

   (A) so that it would be recognized by others as a major European power
   (B) so that it would prosper economically
   (C) so that it could expand its borders to the east
   (D) so that its army and navy could compete with the enemy in war
   (E) so that it would take its cultural, literary, and artistic place among the nations of Europe

142. Empress Maria Theresa of Austria oversaw all the following major reforms EXCEPT

   (A) a thorough centralization of the bureaucracy, following the Prussian model
   (B) promotion to high official positions according to merit rather than birth
   (C) reduction of the peasants' financial and service obligations to the wealthy estate owners
   (D) the passage of laws giving equal protection to all religious groups within the empire
   (E) the secularization and reform of the system of higher education

143. Which of the following had the greatest effect on the balance of power in Europe in the mid-1700s?

   (A) Prussia's swift rise to power
   (B) Russia's expansion into the west
   (C) the three partitions of Poland
   (D) Spain's colonial expansion in the Americas
   (E) Britain's colonial expansion in the Americas

144. Stepan "Stenka" Razin is a significant figure in 17th-century Russian history for

   (A) leading a major popular uprising against landowners and state authority
   (B) engineering the passage of a new criminal and civil law code
   (C) orchestrating a schism in the Eastern Orthodox Church
   (D) being executed by the czar for being a leader of the Old Believers
   (E) leading successful military campaigns against Sweden and Poland

145. What did Austria gain as a result of the Silesian Wars?

(A) Prussian territory

(B) reparations from Prussia

(C) an alliance with Prussia

(D) complete independence from the Holy Roman Empire

(E) Prussian recognition of Hapsburg authority in Austria

146. When Austria took over Hungary in 1687, the treaty between the two provided for all of the following EXCEPT

(A) Austria and Hungary would be jointly ruled by the Austrian emperor

(B) Austria would uphold the current Hungarian constitution

(C) Hungary would be ruled by a hereditary Hapsburg monarchy

(D) Hungary would cede the right to rise up against Austrian rule

(E) Austria would guarantee freedom from religious discrimination to Hungarian Protestants

147. Which was NOT one result of the French victory over Prussia in 1806?

(A) the creation of the Confederation of the Rhine under French administration

(B) a heavy financial burden of reparation assessed on Prussia

(C) a Franco-Prussian alliance against Russia in the invasion of 1812

(D) an increased sense of national unity among the defeated Germans

(E) the sweeping reorganization of the Prussian government along French lines

148. Which was NOT one purpose of the "Grand Embassy" undertaken by Peter the Great and his entourage in 1697–1698?

(A) to investigate the possibility of reuniting the Eastern Orthodox and Roman Catholic churches

(B) to send Russians abroad for study and training

(C) to recruit able and talented Europeans for service in Russia

(D) to establish permanent Russian embassies in European nations

(E) to acquire Western books and to view Western cultural, artistic, and scientific achievements

149. In the period following the Thirty Years' War, all these factors combined
    to keep the Holy Roman Empire weak EXCEPT

    (A) the huge drop in the population that resulted from the war
    (B) inability to establish colonies in the Americas
    (C) legal barriers to efficient or free trade within the empire
    (D) the difficulty of much economic growth in any of the numerous
        small principalities
    (E) linguistic and cultural diversity throughout the empire

Exploration and Colonization from 1492 to the American Revolution

150. Which of the following is NOT a significant European figure
    in the colonization of the Americas?

    (A) Hernán Cortés
    (B) Pedro Menendez de Avilés
    (C) Leif Eriksson
    (D) Walter Raleigh
    (E) John Winthrop

151. As a result of the Seven Years' War, control of Canada passed from

    (A) Britain to France
    (B) Spain to Britain
    (C) Britain to Spain
    (D) France to Britain
    (E) Spain to France

152. Which was the first European nation to sponsor a transatlantic voyage
    of exploration?

    (A) England
    (B) France
    (C) Italy
    (D) Portugal
    (E) Spain

153. Which was NOT one major European motivation for exploration
    of the seas and lands beyond Europe?

    (A) the search for new trading partners and better trade routes
    (B) the desire to become stronger by acquiring colonies
    (C) the lack of opportunity at home
    (D) the zest for religious conversion of so-called heathen populations
    (E) the universal human instinct of curiosity about the unknown

154. The relatively swift conquest of the American empires and tribes was mainly due to the European explorers'
   (A) sophisticated weapons
   (B) superior intelligence
   (C) numerical strength
   (D) religious faith
   (E) literacy

155. What was Portugal's main goal in sailing around Africa to reach India in 1498?
   (A) to colonize India
   (B) to initiate a religious war with the Arabs in the region
   (C) to establish trading posts
   (D) to convert the Indians to Catholicism
   (E) to find a water route to the west by sailing east

156. The French and Indian War began over rival French and British claims to
   (A) Indian territory in the southeast
   (B) the city of New Orleans
   (C) Canadian territory
   (D) colonies along the Atlantic coast of North America
   (E) land in the Ohio River valley

157. The voyage of Ferdinand Magellan is historically significant because his crew members became the first Europeans to
   (A) sail all the way around the globe
   (B) see the Pacific Ocean from the Americas
   (C) establish a viable European colony in the Americas
   (D) explore the interior of North America
   (E) establish contact with the native populations of South America

158. The Dutch profited more than the Portuguese from trade with the Pacific islands for all these reasons EXCEPT
   (A) the Dutch fleet proved militarily superior to the Portuguese
   (B) the Dutch merchant fleet was larger than the Portuguese
   (C) the Dutch paid cash for Asian crops and goods rather than bartering with them
   (D) the Dutch did not try to convert the Asians to Christianity
   (E) Dutch ships were larger and could thus carry more goods per trip

159. Which best explains why the transatlantic trade in African slaves arose during the era of European colonization?

(A) Very few Europeans wanted to travel to the Americas.

(B) A substantial drop in the native American population forced the Europeans to look elsewhere for cheap labor.

(C) Native American peoples refused to work for the Europeans.

(D) Americans were not physically fit for the large-scale farming and mining necessary to make colonization profitable.

(E) Europeans did not regard the native American peoples as suitable targets for exploitation or enforced labor.

160. Francisco Pizarro of Spain led the conquest of which major American civilization?

(A) Aztec

(B) Maya

(C) Inca

(D) Olmec

(E) Toltec

161. The primary French activity in North America in the 16th century was

(A) building major permanent French settlements

(B) fighting battles with the Indian population

(C) fighting a war against the British over colonial territory

(D) establishing a new fur-trading industry

(E) drawing up plans for a canal in the Great Lakes region

162. All of the following are among the significant English or English-sponsored explorers of the era EXCEPT

(A) Sebastian Cabot

(B) Samuel de Champlain

(C) Frances Drake

(D) Henry Hudson

(E) Sir Walter Raleigh

163. Britain's North American colonies rebelled against British rule in the 1770s over the issue of

(A) being denied the privilege of voting on new taxes assessed by Parliament

(B) the loss of territory in the French and Indian War

(C) the significant British military presence throughout the colonies

(D) British regulation of colonial trade

(E) British refusal to validate the various colonial charters

164. The Treaty of Paris that ended the Seven Years' War and the French and Indian War in 1763 ended with France ceding all its North American territory to

(A) Britain and Spain
(B) Spain and Austria
(C) Austria and Britain
(D) Prussia and Britain
(E) Spain and Prussia

165. The success of Portuguese traders in the Pacific was made possible by

(A) the discovery of sea routes by Vasco da Gama
(B) the transatlantic voyages of Christopher Columbus
(C) the opening of the Suez Canal
(D) the distance between Australia and Asia
(E) the self-imposed isolation of Japan

CHAPTER 3

The Era of Political and Intellectual Revolution

The Scientific Revolution

166. Which of the following scientists proved conclusively that the Earth orbited the sun?

    (A) Nicolaus Copernicus
    (B) Tycho Brahe
    (C) Johannes Kepler
    (D) Galileo Galilei
    (E) Isaac Newton

167. On what grounds did Galileo defend his discoveries in the field of astronomy against opposition?

    (A) that he had used the best and most modern scientific equipment
    (B) that what the human eye could see must be the truth
    (C) that priests had no knowledge of astronomy
    (D) that other scientists shared his conclusions
    (E) that his work had been sponsored by the university

168. In what way did the theories of the 17th-century scientists differ from those of the ancients?

    (A) The ancients relied on abstract thought, the moderns on direct observation and experimentation.
    (B) The ancients depended on wealthy patrons to support their studies; the moderns did not.
    (C) The ancients had to publish anonymously to circumvent censorship; the moderns did not.
    (D) The moderns tried to find rational explanations for what they saw in the heavens; the ancients did not.
    (E) The moderns had great difficulty making their discoveries public; the ancients did not.

169. How did the Church react to the discoveries of the Scientific Revolution?

(A) It ignored the discoveries completely.
(B) It felt that the discoveries threatened its own authority.
(C) It began cautiously to sponsor scientific research of its own.
(D) It excommunicated all Catholic scientists.
(E) It enthusiastically supported the new discoveries.

170. Which of the following discoveries revealed that the workings of the universe were governed by mathematical principles that human beings could understand?

(A) the discovery of Jupiter's moons
(B) the discovery of the planets' elliptical orbits
(C) the discovery of the law of gravity
(D) the discovery of the rings of Saturn
(E) the discovery that the planets moved around the sun

171. Galileo is notable for all of the following discoveries EXCEPT

(A) the moons of Jupiter
(B) the law of falling bodies
(C) the mathematical formula for acceleration
(D) sunspots
(E) the principle governing the tides

172. Christiaan Huygens of Holland is notable for all the following achievements EXCEPT

(A) inventing the pendulum clock
(B) explaining the phenomenon of the rainbow
(C) publishing the first paper on the theory of probability
(D) identifying the rings of Saturn
(E) making major contributions to the mathematics of curves

173. The Paris Observatory was the headquarters for all these major 17th-century scientific experiments EXCEPT

(A) the discovery of the moons of Jupiter
(B) the measurement of the exact circumference of the Earth
(C) the measurement of the distance between the Earth and the sun
(D) the verification of early experiments of Danish astronomer Tycho Brahe
(E) the discovery of the satellites of Saturn

174. In his *De Revolutionibus* of 1543, Nicolaus Copernicus advanced the theory that

(A) the Earth orbits the sun
(B) the orbits of the planets are elliptical
(C) the orbits of the planets are irregular
(D) all objects in the universe are in motion
(E) the sun and moon orbit the Earth

175. Which best explains the doctrine of empiricism, which Francis Bacon made a central part of the scientific method in the 17th century?

(A) What can be perceived through the five senses must be the truth.
(B) Truth can be arrived at by means of abstract reasoning.
(C) The ability to think is the proof of independent existence.
(D) Acceptance of the existence of God must be the starting point for any investigation of the workings of the universe.
(E) Science can only progress if religion is left behind.

176. Which best explains why the Church had always supported the scientific theories of Ptolemy and Aristotle?

(A) The theories were literally echoed in passages of the Bible.
(B) The theories had been proved beyond any doubt.
(C) Both men were known to have been profoundly religious.
(D) The theories stated that the Earth, and therefore humankind, was at the center of the universe.
(E) Both men were intellectuals of the highest standing in ancient times.

177. When the Church authorities denied his scientific findings because they contradicted Holy Scripture, Galileo responded

(A) that religious beliefs were mere superstition, while scientific findings were facts
(B) that science and the Bible were necessarily contradictory and incompatible
(C) that science had no relationship to religion
(D) that scientific findings disproved the Bible once and for all
(E) that the Church's interpretation of Scripture must be at fault

178. Which of the following was NOT a significant contributor to the Scientific Revolution?

(A) René Descartes
(B) Galileo Galilei
(C) Edmond Halley
(D) Samuel Pepys
(E) Jean Picard

179. Newton's *Principia Mathematica* (*Mathematical Principles of Natural Philosophy*), published in 1686–1687, was the first book to set forth and explain

(A) astronomy
(B) biology
(C) chemistry
(D) geometry
(E) physics

180. The thinkers of the Scientific Revolution were the first to establish that the shape of the Earth is

(A) a perfect sphere
(B) a sphere slightly flattened at the poles
(C) a sphere slightly elongated at the poles
(D) an irregular shape loosely resembling a sphere
(E) an ellipse

The Enlightenment, or the Age of Reason

181. Which of the following is the best translation of the Enlightenment term *philosophe*?

(A) scholar
(B) revolutionary
(C) reformer
(D) critical thinker
(E) scientist

182. All the *philosophes* of the Enlightenment had which of the following characteristics in common?

(A) They all had the same profession.
(B) They were all French.
(C) They all used the same reasoning process.
(D) They were all pacifists.
(E) They were all self-educated.

183. The *Encyclopédie* is best described as a multi-volume

    (A) philosophical treatise

    (B) rationalist version of the Bible

    (C) source of information on history, science, philosophy, and the arts

    (D) collection of propositions for intellectual, artistic, and religious debate

    (E) treatise on intellectual history from ancient times to the present day

184. *The Spirit of Laws* is historically significant as the first book to argue in favor of

    (A) a government of checks and balances

    (B) a powerful legislative assembly

    (C) rule by direct democracy

    (D) absolute freedom of the press

    (E) the separation of church and state

185. When the title character in Voltaire's *Candide* states at the end of the book that "one must cultivate one's garden," he means

    (A) agricultural workers are the most important members of a society

    (B) people should mind their own business

    (C) all is for the best in the best of all possible worlds

    (D) philosophy should be applied to the solution of practical problems

    (E) everyone must learn to provide for his or her own needs

186. Jean-Jacques Rousseau was alone among the *philosophes* in his belief that the solution to the ills of society was

    (A) universal public education

    (B) the elimination of the man-made structure of social ranks

    (C) philosophical debate among intellectuals

    (D) violent political revolution

    (E) the elimination of hereditary monarchy

187. Which of the following stimulated both the Scientific Revolution and the Enlightenment?

    (A) the application of ancient theories to modern questions

    (B) the creation of new solutions to major social problems

    (C) the approval, support, and sponsorship of the Church

    (D) the design of new, representative systems of government

    (E) the process of critical thinking and drawing conclusions from data

188. Which of the following is NOT one reason why the Enlightenment was centered in France?

(A) French was the common language of educated Europeans of the time.

(B) France had been the dominant power in Europe since its victory in the Thirty Years' War.

(C) France had a representative government and relative religious tolerance.

(D) France's central geographical location made it a convenient gathering place.

(E) France had a longstanding tradition of state support for science, letters, and the arts.

189. The Enlightenment helped to create a climate of opposition throughout the Western world to all of the following EXCEPT

(A) chattel slavery

(B) inequality between men and women

(C) privileges based solely on birth

(D) political tyranny

(E) censorship of the press

190. Why did the *philosophes* regard Britain as an ideal society?

(A) Many of the greatest *philosophes* were born in Britain.

(B) Britain was a major world power in spite of its small size.

(C) British society boasted both relative religious tolerance and a free press.

(D) Britain's government was politically and financially stable.

(E) By the end of the Enlightenment, Britain was already beginning to industrialize.

191. Which of the following does NOT help to explain why Enlightenment ideas had such a strong influence throughout all ranks of French society?

(A) France's literacy rate doubled over the course of the 18th century.

(B) The publishing industry made books, pamphlets, and journals widely and cheaply available.

(C) Gathering places such as coffeehouses and salons fostered public discussion and debate.

(D) Voltaire, Montesquieu, and others wrote entertaining works of fiction that made their arguments accessible to ordinary people.

(E) France was one of the few European nations that had universal, free public education.

192. What did the *philosophes* anticipate for the future of humankind?
   (A) Society would be shaken by violent revolution.
   (B) Life would continue to be a struggle against tyranny and oppression.
   (C) Universal peace and prosperity might truly be achieved.
   (D) Major wars would eventually destroy civilization.
   (E) The future would never be as glorious as the ancient past.

193. Which does NOT describe one manner in which the major literary figures of the Age of Reason responded to censorship in the publishing industry and the press?
   (A) They took up arms against the censors.
   (B) They smuggled their works into Holland or England for publication.
   (C) They published allegorical fiction in which social criticism was implied rather than directly stated.
   (D) They moved to locations where it would be easy to flee over the border if they aroused official anger.
   (E) They expressed their opinions openly and risked the official consequences.

194. Jean-Jacques Rousseau's *Confessions* is considered to anticipate the Romantic movement in literature because
   (A) it is among the first modern autobiographies
   (B) it concentrates on the author's emotions and personality rather than the facts of his life
   (C) it is an autobiography by a literary figure rather than a statesman or monarch
   (D) its main purpose is to criticize society rather than to tell the story of the author's life
   (E) it attempts to portray its author in the most favorable possible light

195. Which of the following is NOT considered one of the major thinkers of the Enlightenment, or the Age of Reason?
   (A) Jean le Rond d'Alembert
   (B) John Locke
   (C) Benjamin Franklin
   (D) Antonio Gramsci
   (E) Voltaire

The French Revolution and the Napoleonic Wars

196. All of the following contributed to the outbreak of revolution in France EXCEPT

(A) the success of revolutions in Britain and North America
(B) growing desire for a political voice among the aristocracy
(C) widespread crop failure and food shortages leading to famine
(D) higher taxes on the common people and higher prices for all
(E) the spread of Enlightenment ideas of freedom and equality

197. Which best describes the three groups that comprised the Estates General?

(A) clergy, aristocracy, commoners
(B) aristocracy, military, commoners
(C) clergy, landowners, tenants
(D) wealthy clergy and aristocracy, wealthy merchants and professionals, poor clergy and commoners
(E) upper nobility, military officers, and high-ranking clergy; lower nobility, wealthy merchants, and professionals; common soldiers, poor clergy, and working people

198. Which of the following best explains why France had so much difficulty establishing a functioning republican government?

(A) No model of a republican government existed that France might have studied and imitated.
(B) The military was too absorbed in foreign wars to help establish domestic order.
(C) The citizens would only support the creation of a workers' state.
(D) The people wanted to establish a constitutional monarchy.
(E) France had no experienced legislative assembly on which to build.

199. All of the following help to account for the downfall of Napoleon EXCEPT

(A) his successful conquests had made all other European nations unite against France
(B) his responsibilities as emperor distracted him from his military campaigns
(C) the thousands of foreign mercenaries in the Grand Army did not care much about either Napoleon or France
(D) he failed to set coherent domestic policies or to create a smoothly functioning bureaucracy
(E) French nationalism inspired nationalism in the nations France attacked and invaded

200. Why did Louis XVI summon the Estates General in the spring of 1789?

    (A) to enlist support for a major program of social reform

    (B) to seek advice on how to solve the financial crisis

    (C) to work with the deputies on creating a new national constitution

    (D) to explain that he intended to dissolve the legislature for good

    (E) to ask the deputies to appoint a few leaders as chief ministers to the king

201. The Tennis-Court Oath led immediately to which of the following?

    (A) the end of the famine and food shortages

    (B) the imprisonment of the royal family

    (C) the legal dissolution of the monarchy

    (D) royal agreement to certain civil rights and tax reforms

    (E) eligibility for high office based on merit rather than rank

202. The people of Paris stormed the Bastille for all these reasons EXCEPT

    (A) they regarded it as a hated symbol of royal oppression

    (B) they wanted the weapons that were stored there

    (C) they intended to use it as a defensive fort during the uprising

    (D) they wanted to take revenge on the officials in charge of it

    (E) they did not want to wait any longer for news from Versailles

203. Which best describes the Declaration of the Rights of Man and of the Citizen?

    (A) It describes the form of the future French government in specific detail.

    (B) It sets forth specific civil and legal rights and responsibilities of the people.

    (C) It proclaims the end of the monarchy and the beginning of the republic.

    (D) It explains the reasons for the continued uprisings of the people of Paris.

    (E) It confers imperial authority on the First Consul of France.

204. Those who supported a constitutional monarchy rather than a republic began to change their minds when

    (A) the king was caught in an attempted escape from prison

    (B) the women of Paris marched on Versailles

    (C) the people of Paris stormed the Bastille

    (D) the aristocrats began fleeing the country in large numbers

    (E) the military indicated its support for the people

205. On what grounds did the National Convention call for the execution of Louis XVI?

(A) that he was a traitor to the Revolution

(B) that he was married to an Austrian princess

(C) that he had refused to sign the Declaration of the Rights of Man and of the Citizen

(D) that before 1789, he had ruled France as an absolute monarch

(E) that he had failed to provide France with a legitimate heir to the throne

206. Which best describes the Jacobins and Girondins of the early 1790s?

(A) formally organized, mainstream political parties

(B) groups of radicals who wanted to overthrow the National Convention

(C) informal clubs for deputies and intellectuals who shared a political philosophy

(D) military factions who took opposing views of Napoleon

(E) groups of aristocrats scheming to overthrow the Revolution

207. Which of the following is NOT one reason the Directory failed to become a strong, functional legislature?

(A) Its deputies could not agree on what kind of government was best for France.

(B) Its deputies were elected or appointed by local assemblies throughout France.

(C) It tried to eliminate the Catholic Church as a rival to its own authority.

(D) It actively discriminated against members of the former First Estate.

(E) It denied all civil and political rights to members of the former Second Estate.

208. Which accurately describes the Code Napoleon?

(A) a law code that set forth the basic rights and responsibilities of the citizens

(B) the reorganization of the civil service

(C) the creation of France's first public-school system

(D) an agreement with the pope that reestablished the Catholic Church in France

(E) a declaration that Napoleon was hereditary emperor of the French for life

209. During the Napoleonic Wars, Britain first sent troops to mainland Europe in support of

(A) Austria
(B) the Holy Roman Empire
(C) Italy
(D) Russia
(E) Spain

210. All of the following helped to forge unity between the French aristocracy and the wealthiest commoners in the pre-Revolutionary years EXCEPT

(A) both were discontented with having no voice in the government
(B) many wealthy commoners attained noble titles by purchase or reward
(C) both were concerned with the preservation and protection of property rights
(D) wealthy commoners often married aristocrats
(E) both supported major social and political reform

211. The rule of the Committee of Public Safety was characterized by all of the following EXCEPT

(A) support for popular revolutions throughout Europe
(B) government control of prices
(C) nationalization of small businesses
(D) mass executions of aristocrats and other alleged enemies of the state
(E) enlargement of the army

212. Napoleon's important domestic reforms include all of the following EXCEPT

(A) the establishment of a national banking system
(B) the reestablishment of the Catholic Church in France
(C) the creation of the nation's first public-school system
(D) the introduction of full civil and legal equality for women
(E) the division of France into local-government units called *départements*

213. Which of the following nations was neither invaded by France, nor forced into a French alliance?

(A) Austria
(B) Britain
(C) Prussia
(D) Russia
(E) Spain

214. Napoleon issued the Berlin and Milan decrees of 1806 and 1807 with the intention of

(A) creating a unified Italian state under French rule
(B) creating a unified German state under French rule
(C) forming alliances with Germany and Italy
(D) blocking British exports to continental Europe
(E) forcing young men throughout the French Empire to enlist in the Grand Army

215. Which best describes the military strategy that Napoleon used with almost total success up to the invasion of Russia in 1812?

(A) to remain on the defensive, forcing the enemy to come into the open
(B) to rely on his infantry to wage a series of guerrilla-style ambushes
(C) to occupy the capital city and thus force the monarch to come to terms
(D) to command his troops to lay waste to all the country through which they marched
(E) to recruit vast numbers of foreign mercenaries to supplement the French troops

216. Which of the following is NOT one cause of Napoleon's defeat in Russia?

(A) The Russians evacuated Moscow and burned it to the ground.
(B) Russian troops and their allies together outnumbered the Grand Army troops.
(C) Czar Alexander I refused to discuss terms with Napoleon.
(D) The Grand Army was not prepared for the Russian winter.
(E) The Russian steppes offered little food and water for the invading troops.

217. Which form of government did Spain establish or reestablish as a result of defeating Napoleon in 1814?

(A) an absolute monarchy
(B) a constitutional monarchy
(C) a representative republic with an elected president
(D) a Socialist state with some democratic features
(E) a military dictatorship

218. Which event interrupted the deliberations at the Congress of Vienna?

- (A) the French retreat and rout in Russia
- (B) the creation of the Confederation of the Rhine
- (C) the unification of Germany
- (D) Napoleon's escape from Elba and return to France
- (E) Napoleon's exile to Elba

219. Napoleon's European opponents united against him largely in order to

- (A) establish democratic rule in France
- (B) restore the balance of power in Europe
- (C) take over France and its territories
- (D) end the alliance between France and the United States
- (E) bring about the unification of the German states

220. The leaders at the Congress of Vienna achieved all the following EXCEPT

- (A) turning over control of new territories to several of the victorious nations
- (B) strengthening the union of the German-speaking states as a check on French power
- (C) agreeing to meet when necessary to maintain peace treaties and settle new issues as they arose
- (D) expressing belief in and pledging support for the system of legitimate hereditary monarchy
- (E) redrawing the borders of the minor European states along ethnic/linguistic/cultural lines

221. Why did Napoleon sign a concordat with the pope in 1801?

- (A) He did not believe that religious observance was important to the state.
- (B) He believed that a traditional form of worship was important to the people.
- (C) He had no personal religious convictions of his own.
- (D) He desired an alliance between France and the Papal States.
- (E) He believed that the people of France should enjoy religious liberty.

222. Napoleon's final defeat on the battlefield took place at

- (A) Austerlitz
- (B) Borodino
- (C) Moscow
- (D) Salamanca
- (E) Waterloo

223. Which two groups united to swear the Tennis-Court Oath and create the National Assembly in 1789?

(A) members of the First and Second estates
(B) members of the First and Third estates
(C) members of the Second and Third estates
(D) the National Guard and the workers
(E) the workers and the unemployed poor

224. Why did the women of Paris march on Versailles in 1789?

(A) to arrest and imprison the royal family
(B) to steal any valuables they could lay hands on
(C) to demand that the king end the severe food shortage
(D) to burn Versailles to the ground
(E) to declare the establishment of a workers' state

225. Which form of government did France establish in the wake of Napoleon's fall from power?

(A) a military dictatorship
(B) a constitutional monarchy
(C) a democratic republic
(D) a workers' state
(E) a multinational empire

The Industrial Revolution

226. All these factors delayed the development of manufacturing and industry on the European continent EXCEPT

(A) the political and economic upheaval caused by the Napoleonic Wars
(B) the lack of modern scientific knowledge and skills
(C) the strong political and territorial rivalry among European nations
(D) the lack of political influence in the mercantile middle class in most nations
(E) the lack of free-trade agreements among nations

227. Industrial development in the Mediterranean relied on water and steam power because the region lacked which natural resource?

(A) natural gas
(B) oil
(C) coal
(D) timber
(E) electricity

228. The enclosure movement that began in Britain during the Industrial Revolution had all the following effects EXCEPT

(A) landlords began establishing factories on their estates
(B) landlords fenced in their privately owned lands for their own use
(C) villagers and tenants could no longer grow crops in the open fields
(D) thousands of country people migrated to the cities to find work for wages
(E) landlords began experimenting with agricultural innovations that made their estates profitable

229. British food production soared in the late 18th century partly because Jethro Tull's agricultural innovations improved farmers' ability to

(A) diversify their crops
(B) sow their seed
(C) rotate their crops
(D) fertilize their fields
(E) harvest their crops

230. When World War I broke out in 1914, which European nation had the most industrialized economy?

(A) Austria
(B) Britain
(C) France
(D) Germany
(E) Russia

231. All of the following inventions brought major changes to Britain's textile industry in the 18th century EXCEPT

(A) the flying shuttle
(B) the steam-powered loom
(C) the development of the railway
(D) the spinning mule
(E) the water frame

232. Which issue was at the root of business owners' opposition to government regulation and the formation of trade unions?

(A) child labor
(B) health benefits
(C) political influence
(D) profits
(E) property rights

233. The Industrial Revolution began and flourished in Britain long before it spread to the European continent for all these reasons EXCEPT

(A) no part of the Napoleonic Wars had been fought on British soil
(B) Britain was financially prosperous and politically stable
(C) the British climate was temperate during most of the year
(D) Britain and the United States collaborated on many inventions
(E) Britain was connected by a network of rivers and canals

234. When did the legalization of trade unions in industrialized European nations begin?

(A) in the mid-18th century
(B) in the late 18th century
(C) in the early 19th century
(D) in the mid-19th century
(E) in the late 19th century

235. Which industry was the mainstay of the British economy both before and after the Industrial Revolution?

(A) the textile industry
(B) the livestock industry
(C) the agricultural industry
(D) the shipbuilding industry
(E) the mining industry

236. How did industrialization affect the economies of the European nations in the 19th century?

(A) Expenditure on machinery, roads and railways, and factories created heavy national debt.
(B) People began buying on credit on a regular basis.
(C) The government saw a sharp rise in revenue from taxes.
(D) Individuals across all social classes saw a substantial rise in their incomes.
(E) Profits rose because trade regulations were abolished throughout Europe.

237. Which of the following was the most important factor in a nation's ability to industrialize?

(A) its natural resources
(B) its economy
(C) its political relations with neighboring nations
(D) its available population of workers
(E) its proximity to major railroads

238. How did the development of the railway system increase the profits of the manufacturing industry?

(A) by reducing the time and cost of shipping goods
(B) by making passenger travel faster and cheaper
(C) by bringing industrialization to isolated regions
(D) by employing thousands of workers
(E) by making it possible to ship goods at any time of year

239. What was the most important source of power for a European factory worker in the late 19th century?

(A) the right to vote in national elections
(B) ownership of stock in the company he or she worked for
(C) membership in a trade union
(D) the freedom to rise in a company through merit-based promotion
(E) the right to organize violent public demonstrations against the owners

240. Influential social scientists Jeremy Bentham and John Stuart Mill argued that

(A) when one person's situation deteriorates, the rest of the community gains from that person's losses
(B) when one person's situation improves, the entire community is that much better off
(C) each person should always do what appears to be to his or her own advantage
(D) each person should always do what appears most likely to benefit others
(E) industrialization was a necessary evil that must be carefully monitored by the public

The Austrian and Russian Empires in the 19th Century

241. All of the following are true of both Austrian and Russian empires in the wake of the Congress of Vienna EXCEPT

(A) both agreed to suppress popular insurrection wherever it arose in Europe
(B) neither favored any element of popular representation in the national government
(C) neither was willing to consider emancipation of the peasants in the empire
(D) both were ruled by monarchs who believed in the divine right of kings
(E) neither had any sympathy with the political philosophy of liberalism

242. Which element of the Russian population was the moving spirit behind the Decembrist Revolution of 1825?

(A) the wealthy landowners
(B) the liberal and nationalist intellectuals
(C) the urban workers
(D) the serfs, free peasants, and small farmers
(E) the military

243. Which of the following states did NOT become part of the Austrian Empire as a result of the Congress of Vienna?

(A) Bohemia
(B) Croatia
(C) Hungary
(D) Serbia
(E) Transylvania

244. In 1867, Emperor Francis Joseph of Austria responded to demands for Hungarian independence by

(A) cracking down on the Hungarians and revoking many of their civil rights
(B) granting Hungary a certain measure of self-government within the empire
(C) forcing the Hungarians to adopt the German language and Austrian culture and customs
(D) making Hungary a fully independent nation
(E) laying the question of Hungarian self-rule before an international committee

245. When Czar Alexander II determined to emancipate the serfs, he faced all the following issues EXCEPT

(A) the probable outbreak of a bloody and brutal civil war
(B) providing the freed serfs with land of their own
(C) compensating the landlords for the loss of their serfs
(D) making necessary changes to the system of local government
(E) changing the law codes to give the serfs the legal rights of free Russians

246. Austrian minister Klemens von Metternich pursued all the following goals at the Congress of Vienna EXCEPT

- (A) to unite the Austrian Empire into one unbroken landmass
- (B) to achieve constitutional systems of government throughout Europe
- (C) to keep Italy subordinate to Austria
- (D) to arrange for Austrian control of the confederation of small German states
- (E) to ensure a balance of European power by dealing reasonably with France

247. All of the following contributed significantly to political and social reform under Czar Alexander II of Russia EXCEPT

- (A) Russia's defeat in the Crimean War
- (B) widespread fear of possible peasant insurrection
- (C) the spread of liberal ideas among the educated classes
- (D) the rising costs to landowners of maintaining their serfs
- (E) corruption within the Orthodox Church

248. All of the following made significant contributions to the "golden age" of Russian literature in the 19th century EXCEPT

- (A) Nikolai Gogol
- (B) Boris Pasternak
- (C) Alexander Pushkin
- (D) Leo Tolstoy
- (E) Ivan Turgenev

249. Which of the following did NOT contribute to insurrection in Russia in 1825?

- (A) the establishment of censorship of the university curriculum
- (B) Russia's membership in the Holy Alliance of 1815
- (C) the creation in 1821 of a secret state police force
- (D) the abandonment of an ambitious plan to liberate the serfs
- (E) a sharp rise in taxes to cover the costs of the war against Napoleon

250. According to Austrian chief minister Klemens von Metternich, which was the most important political principle in 19th-century Europe?

- (A) legitimacy
- (B) populism
- (C) revolution
- (D) imperialism
- (E) democracy

251. All of the following happened as direct results of the Austrian uprisings of 1848 EXCEPT

(A) the dismissal of chief minister Klemens von Metternich from office
(B) the opening of a popularly elected Viennese *Reichstag* (parliament)
(C) the passage of a new, liberal constitution
(D) the emancipation of all peasants throughout the empire
(E) the replacement of Emperor Ferdinand I with his nephew Francis Joseph

252. Czar Nicholas I presided over all the following major reforms EXCEPT

(A) the creation of a new civil and criminal law code
(B) the reform of domestic financial policies
(C) the granting of local self-government to peasant villages
(D) a crackdown on certain privileges of the nobility
(E) the elimination of censorship of the press and the arts

253. The Crimean War involved all of the following issues EXCEPT

(A) Ottoman Turkish attempts to expand into Europe by marching on Vienna
(B) France's insistence on recovering control over certain holy sites in Palestine
(C) Austrian objections to a Russian invasion of Turkey through the Balkans
(D) British willingness to support the Ottoman Turks if war broke out
(E) Russian desire to take over Ottoman territory along the Danube

254. Which best describes the goal of the Decembrist revolutionaries in Russia?

(A) political reform
(B) religious reform
(C) social reform
(D) bureaucratic reform
(E) agricultural reform

255. In which of the following aspects of 19th-century Austrian affairs did the Rothschild family play a major role?

(A) in the military
(B) in finance and industry
(C) in education
(D) in the civil service
(E) in the Church

256. Which of the following staged an unsuccessful rebellion against Czar Nicholas I in 1830–1831?

(A) Austria
(B) Greece
(C) Poland
(D) the Russian workers
(E) the Russian peasants

257. In the era leading up to the 1905 revolution, the Russian government had none of the following EXCEPT

(A) legitimate, organized political parties
(B) a criminal and civil law code
(C) the right to vote in national elections
(D) recognized trade unions or workers' associations
(E) a representative legislature

258. Which of the following proved to be an explosive force in the Austrian Empire in the 1840s?

(A) liberalism
(B) conservatism
(C) nationalism
(D) Socialism
(E) Marxism

Nineteenth-Century Political Movements and Revolutions

259. Which best defines the Romantic movement in literature and the arts?

(A) It emphasized the individual personality of the artist.
(B) It celebrated content rather than form.
(C) It emphasized romantic love as the favorite topic.
(D) It encouraged creativity within fixed literary, artistic, and musical forms.
(E) It was heavily if not primarily a German cultural phenomenon.

260. The primary cause of the political turmoil that characterized 19th-century France was

(A) its lack of a written constitution
(B) its lack of competent monarchs
(C) disagreement among political parties and factions
(D) French defeat in the war with Prussia
(E) the closing of the national workshops

261. Which was most responsible for determining the outcome of the Franco-Prussian War?

(A) French diplomatic efforts
(B) Prussian diplomatic efforts
(C) French military superiority
(D) German military superiority
(E) factionalism among the French leaders

262. Which two British political parties joined forces in the late 19th century to create the Liberal Party?

(A) Whigs and Tories
(B) Tories and Conservatives
(C) Conservatives and Labour
(D) Labour and Radicals
(E) Radicals and Whigs

263. Which Italian kingdom(s) took the lead in the unification of the nation of Italy?

(A) Lombardy, Venice, and the Tyrol
(B) Naples and Sicily
(C) Parma and Modena
(D) Rome
(E) Sardinia and Piedmont

264. Which is NOT a social reform passed by the newly formed Liberal Party of Britain under its leader, Prime Minister William Gladstone?

(A) Public education was made free and compulsory.
(B) Farm workers were granted the right to vote.
(C) Public housing was provided at low cost for urban workers.
(D) The secret ballot was introduced.
(E) The basis for promotion in the military was changed from birth to merit.

265. Which of the following was most responsible for bringing about an era of reform in Britain in the early 1800s?

(A) massive, violent workers' riots and demonstrations
(B) political conspiracies
(C) the death of George IV and the subsequent coronation of William IV
(D) constant agitation in the newspapers and journals
(E) widespread economic depression

266. Which group would be the most likely to support government by
a constitutional monarch working with a popularly elected legislature?

(A) conservatives
(B) liberals
(C) Marxists
(D) nationalists
(E) Socialists

267. Which best explains why Prussia provoked France into declaring war
in 1870?

(A) to force the French king to abdicate
(B) to extract massive financial compensation from France
(C) to make Austria part of a new German confederation
(D) to forge an alliance between Prussia and the southern German states
(E) to create a vast Franco-German empire

268. Who was Count Camillo di Cavour's most important ally in driving
the Austrians out of northern Italy in 1860?

(A) Britain
(B) France
(C) Hungary
(D) Prussia
(E) Poland

269. In *The Communist Manifesto*, Karl Marx and Friedrich Engels argued
all of the following EXCEPT

(A) the working class should overthrow society by means of violence
(B) all people belonged to one of two classes, the proletariat (workers)
or the bourgeoisie (owners and managers)
(C) the worker was the most valuable member of society because he
or she produced goods
(D) workers need only rise up against conservative governments
(E) social and economic status, not nationality, was the most important
bond people had with one another

270. The goals of the revolutionaries of 1848 included all of the following
EXCEPT

(A) students' and liberals' demands for a greater voice in government
(B) workers' demands for regulation or reform of industry
(C) liberals' demands for freedom of choice in religious worship
(D) nationalists' desire to achieve self-determination
(E) workers' protests against economic conditions

271. Nationalism would most likely prove to be a divisive force in which of the following nation-states?

(A) one that had a written constitution and a bill of individual rights
(B) one whose people shared a common linguistic and cultural heritage
(C) one that was heavily industrialized and had large urban populations
(D) one that had a balance of powers in the government
(E) one that contained large and vocal ethnic minority groups

272. Pope Pius IX opposed the unification of Italy because

(A) unification would rob him of his authority as a head of state
(B) unification would eliminate the Church's authority in Italy
(C) the leaders intended to establish a representative republican government
(D) the leaders intended to establish a hereditary monarchy
(E) he was afraid that too many lives would be lost in the process of unification

273. Which best describes the political trend in Britain during the 19th century?

(A) conservative
(B) Marxist
(C) repressive
(D) reformist
(E) Socialist

274. Which German province became the core of the newly unified German state in 1871?

(A) Alsace
(B) Bavaria
(C) Hanover
(D) Hesse
(E) Prussia

275. Which of the following events precipitated the fall of Louis Napoleon (also known as Napoleon III)?

(A) the Paris Commune
(B) the Franco-Prussian War
(C) the Revolution of 1830
(D) the Revolution of 1848
(E) the June Days

276. Which of the following is NOT a prominent writer or composer of the Romantic movement that swept across Europe during the 19th century?

(A) Johannes Brahms of Germany
(B) George Sand of France
(C) Mary Wollstonecraft Shelley of England
(D) Giuseppe Verdi of Italy
(E) William Butler Yeats of Ireland

277. Which best describes the overall outcome of the revolutions of 1848?

(A) National borders were redrawn across Europe along ethnic-cultural lines.
(B) The old regimes of Europe continued as they had before the revolutions.
(C) Liberal reforms were passed in various European nations.
(D) A new era of social and economic repression began across Europe.
(E) The people of Europe emerged strongly united across national lines.

278. Which of the following does NOT correctly describe the conservative political philosophy in 19th-century Europe?

(A) belief that it was the government's duty to protect the poorest citizens
(B) opposition to freedom of the press
(C) belief that citizens of birth and education should have some voice in the government
(D) belief in a strong, hereditary monarchy
(E) support for a written constitution

279. Giuseppe Garibaldi is best described as

(A) a popular republican leader
(B) a moderate monarchist
(C) a liberal intellectual
(D) a conservative minister of state
(E) a radical Socialist

280. Nineteenth-century European liberals believed that the strongest branch of the government should be

(A) the bureaucracy or civil service
(B) the constitutional monarch
(C) the freely elected legislature
(D) the military
(E) the national judiciary

281. The term *Realpolitik*, which is closely identified with the policies of German minister Otto von Bismarck, is best defined as
    (A) pragmatism
    (B) warmongering
    (C) appeasement
    (D) benevolent despotism
    (E) pacifism

282. The monarch of the newly united Germany assumed the title *kaiser* to suggest that Germany was, symbolically, a rebirth of
    (A) the Austrian Empire
    (B) the British Empire
    (C) the Ottoman Empire
    (D) the Roman Empire
    (E) the Russian Empire

283. Both Otto von Bismarck of Germany and Count Camillo di Cavour of Italy can be described as
    (A) republicans
    (B) democrats
    (C) conservatives
    (D) Socialists
    (E) military dictators

284. In 1821, the most conservative among the great powers supported a popular uprising in
    (A) Belgium
    (B) Greece
    (C) Italy
    (D) Poland
    (E) Spain

285. Which best describes the legislature of the newly established nation-state of Germany as of the early 1870s?

(A) a unicameral assembly of popularly elected representatives

(B) a unicameral assembly of hereditary nobles who inherited their seats

(C) a unicameral assembly, half royally appointed ministers and half popularly elected representatives

(D) a bicameral congress with one house of popularly elected representatives and one house of hereditary nobles who inherited their seats

(E) a bicameral congress with one house of royally appointed ministers and one house of popularly elected representatives

286. Which 19th-century "-ism" was farthest to the left of the political spectrum?

(A) conservatism

(B) liberalism

(C) Marxism

(D) monarchism

(E) republicanism

287. What was the result of the Greek insurrection against Otto of Bavaria in 1843?

(A) a severe military crackdown on the rebels

(B) a shift toward a more liberal form of government

(C) a tightening of the conservative control of the government

(D) the substitution of a freely elected Greek ruler for the foreign king

(E) a change in Greece's status from monarchy to protectorate

288. The term *Risorgimento* refers to which 19th-century phenomenon?

(A) the rise of nationalism throughout Italy

(B) the triumph of conservatism in Spain

(C) the brief period of an independent Republic of Paris

(D) the war for independence in Greece

(E) the rebellion of various groups within the Austrian Empire

289. Otto von Bismarck achieved his goal of uniting Germany by means of a war against

(A) Britain
(B) France
(C) Austria
(D) Russia
(E) Spain

290. In 19th-century Spain, which of the following was the least powerful?

(A) the monarch
(B) the landowners
(C) the Church
(D) the wealthy middle class
(E) the military

291. Which of the following does NOT help to explain the near-universal opposition with which the ideas of Karl Marx were greeted when he first published them?

(A) Conservatives opposed Marx because he wanted to overturn the traditional social order that they supported.
(B) Liberals opposed Marx because he did not share their reservations about participation in government by the masses.
(C) Nationalists scorned Marx because he believed that what united people was their socioeconomic status, not their ethnic background.
(D) Capitalists regarded Marx as the enemy because he asserted that they had no right to run their own factories as they saw fit.
(E) Socialists opposed Marx because he did not believe in private ownership of business and industry.

292. Which was NOT the site of a major political uprising in 1848?

(A) Austria-Hungary
(B) France
(C) Ireland
(D) Italy
(E) Prussia

293. Nineteenth-century British reforms included all of the following EXCEPT

(A) the establishment of Britain's first national police force
(B) the granting of full civil and political rights to Roman Catholics
(C) the redistribution of seats in Parliament in proportion with the actual population
(D) the passage of child labor laws
(E) the passage of a bill granting women age 21 and over the right to vote

294. During the 19th century, liberals and conservatives agreed on which of the following?

(A) Hereditary monarchy was the ideal form of government.
(B) The lower classes should have no voice in the government.
(C) The separation of powers was essential to good government.
(D) The government must allow universal freedom of speech and of the press.
(E) A good government must have a popularly elected legislature.

295. The Holy Alliance of 1815 was an international agreement to

(A) work together to suppress popular uprisings wherever they occurred
(B) come to the defense of any nation that was attacked by another nation
(C) restore the Catholic Church to its former position of supreme authority in Europe
(D) work together to depose any ruler who did not profess a Christian religion
(E) support popular insurrection against autocratic governments

CHAPTER 4

Empire Building
and World War

Building Empires in Asia and Africa

296. Britain overcame its negative trade balance with China in the 1800s
by importing

(A) cotton
(B) opium
(C) porcelain
(D) silver
(E) tea

297. The Opium Wars exemplify which of the following effects
of the Industrial Revolution?

(A) Republican governments took every opportunity to spread
democracy.
(B) Large nations were invariably able to overpower and colonize
smaller ones.
(C) Modern weapons enabled industrial nations to subjugate
traditional civilizations.
(D) Social revolutions began to depose absolute monarchs.
(E) Nations began to rely on diplomatic negotiations rather
than immediately resorting to force of arms.

298. In 1883, which nation took over a group of Southeast Asian states
that it referred to collectively as Indochina?

(A) Britain
(B) France
(C) Germany
(D) the Netherlands
(E) Portugal

299. What was Britain's primary reason for invading Egypt and imposing protectorate status on it in the late 19th century?

(A) to ensure itself an ally among the Arab nations
(B) to monitor and control Egypt's relations with other African colonies
(C) to achieve financial control over the Suez Canal
(D) to establish and enforce a trade monopoly on Egyptian cotton
(E) to develop Egypt into a modern parliamentary republic

300. In the 19th century, European nations entered into an age of colonial expansion for all these reasons EXCEPT

(A) to reap economic profits from favorable trade agreements
(B) to keep pace with the expansion of other European empires
(C) to gain new converts for their churches and new soldiers for their armies
(D) to impose European cultures on populations the Europeans regarded as uncivilized
(E) to explore and investigate the unknown

301. Which Southeast Asian nation remained independent throughout the era of 19th-century European colonization in the Pacific?

(A) Burma
(B) Java
(C) Siam
(D) Singapore
(E) Vietnam

302. Rural Africans living in the interior were less affected by European colonization than coastal and urban Africans because

(A) they were economically poorer
(B) they were not as well educated
(C) they were not as easily intimidated
(D) they were not geographically accessible
(E) they were less hospitable and trusting

303. During which of the following military conflicts did the British succeed in driving the French out of India?

(A) the Seven Years' War
(B) the Sino-Japanese War
(C) the Sepoy Mutiny
(D) World War I
(E) World War II

304. In the process of establishing control over the Suez Canal, Britain made all of the following into protectorates or colonies EXCEPT

(A) Egypt
(B) Libya
(C) Nigeria
(D) Rhodesia
(E) Sudan

305. Which European nation did NOT amass huge profits from the transatlantic trade in African slaves during the 18th century?

(A) Britain
(B) France
(C) Italy
(D) the Netherlands
(E) Portugal

306. Which is NOT one of the ways in which European missionaries to Africa brought substantial, meaningful improvements with them?

(A) They distributed medicines, doctored and nursed the sick, and trained the Africans to do the same.
(B) They worked to establish representative governments in the colonies.
(C) They created the first written versions of tribal languages and taught the Africans to read and write them.
(D) They pushed for the termination of what they considered barbaric practices, such as polygamy and human sacrifice.
(E) They gained the Africans' respect and regard by assimilating into their cultures.

307. Why did 18th-century Europeans have little difficulty enlisting Africans to sell other Africans into slavery?

(A) African tribes often regarded one another as hostile foreign populations.
(B) Europeans lied to the African captors about the ultimate fate of those who were sold.
(C) Africans felt that it was wise not to antagonize the European invaders by refusing to help them.
(D) African captors believed they were helping their captives gain access to good opportunities overseas.
(E) African tribes often looked to the Europeans to protect them from neighboring tribes.

308. Sub-Saharan Africa was especially tempting to European imperialists because it was rich in all of the following EXCEPT

(A) diamonds
(B) gold
(C) rubber
(D) coffee
(E) maize

309. In the late 1800s, all of the following European nations established spheres of influence in China EXCEPT

(A) Austria
(B) Britain
(C) France
(D) Germany
(E) Russia

310. The Sepoy Mutiny of 1857 is best described as

(A) a wave of armed rebellions in the military and popular uprisings against British rule in central and northeastern India
(B) a battle between the Dutch and British over control of South Africa and the Orange Free State
(C) a struggle over favored-trade status between China on one side and Britain, France, and Germany on the other
(D) the armed conflict between British and French that resulted in the French abandoning their claim to India
(E) a series of popular uprisings against colonial rule throughout sub-Saharan Africa

World War I: From the Buildup to the Aftermath

311. Which of the following does NOT accurately characterize Germany in the first decade of the 20th century?

(A) largest industrial output in Europe
(B) aggressive foreign policy
(C) continual buildup of the armed forces
(D) economically overextended
(E) strongly nationalist

312. Among them, the victorious leaders brought all the following—sometimes conflicting—goals to the conference table at Versailles in 1918 EXCEPT

(A) to establish a lasting peace in Europe
(B) to regain control over specific territory
(C) to abolish trade barriers between nations
(D) to restore the balance of power
(E) to punish and humiliate Germany

313. Which of the combatants from World War I did NOT take part in the Versailles peace conference?

(A) Britain
(B) France
(C) Germany
(D) Italy
(E) Russia

314. By 1900, which of the following had become the greatest source of concern to the British government?

(A) the success of industrialization in Russia
(B) Austria's annexation of Bosnia-Herzegovina
(C) the steady buildup of the German navy
(D) uprisings in British colonies in the Middle East
(E) the possibility of Polish independence

315. All these weapons were first used in World War I EXCEPT

(A) the armored tank
(B) poison gas
(C) the submarine or U-boat
(D) the atomic bomb
(E) the machine gun

316. Which best explains why neither side ever gained any real advantage in the trench war fought on the Western Front?

(A) The weapons of the time combined with the terrain made it impossible to attack effectively.
(B) The climate on the Western Front was sweltering in summer and freezing in winter.
(C) Too many soldiers on both sides were shellshock victims.
(D) Soldiers on both sides were required to serve too many consecutive days without relief.
(E) The skilled commanders on both sides were concentrating their attention on the Eastern Front.

317. Which historical event caused the abrupt withdrawal of one of the major combatants in the war?
(A) the interception of the Zimmerman telegram
(B) the sinking of the *Lusitania*
(C) the Bolshevik Revolution
(D) the Battle of the Marne
(E) the failure of the Schlieffen Plan

318. Which accurately describes the German war plan, also called the Schlieffen Plan?
(A) to conduct a two-front war against France and Russia
(B) to conquer France swiftly at the start, then turn east to attack Russia
(C) to invade and conquer Russia first, then to march on France
(D) to prevent the United States from coming to France's aid
(E) to prevent Britain from coming to France's aid by demolishing the British navy

319. Which accurately describes the national alliances at the start of the war?
(A) Britain and France against Austria and Germany
(B) Britain, France, and Russia against Austria and Germany
(C) Britain, France, Russia, and the United States against Austria, Germany, and Italy
(D) Britain and France against Russia and Germany
(E) Britain and Russia against France and Germany

320. Germany declared war in 1914 because
(A) Austria annexed Bosnia-Herzegovina
(B) Serbian Gavrilo Princip assassinated Austrian Archduke Franz Ferdinand and Archduchess Sophie
(C) Russia began mobilizing against Austria
(D) Britain agreed to support France in the case of a German invasion
(E) Austria invaded Serbia

321. What was Gavrilo Princip's motive for shooting Archduke Franz Ferdinand and Archduchess Sophie of Austria?
(A) religion
(B) anarchism
(C) nationalism
(D) liberalism
(E) imperialism

322. The Schlieffen Plan failed when Germany lost the war's first major battle at

    (A) Brest-Litovsk
    (B) Verdun
    (C) Ypres
    (D) the Somme
    (E) the Marne

323. The Treaty of Versailles called for all of the following EXCEPT

    (A) the independence of Poland
    (B) the creation of the state of Czechoslovakia
    (C) the turnover of Alsace and Lorraine from Germany to France
    (D) the occupation of Germany by Allied troops
    (E) the reduction of Germany's military forces

324. Which best describes the League of Nations?

    (A) an international economic union that provided for free trade among member nations
    (B) a forum in which leaders could discuss and resolve international conflicts peacefully
    (C) an army that would always be ready to defend any nation that was attacked or invaded
    (D) a group of international scientists who would develop new, more efficient weapons
    (E) an international court that would try and judge accused war criminals

325. When Kaiser Wilhelm II of Germany abdicated at the end of the war, which of the following took over the German government?

    (A) the German Nazi Party
    (B) the Comintern (International Communist Party)
    (C) the Allied occupation forces
    (D) the German Social Democratic Party
    (E) the League of Nations

326. The tide of war turned in favor of the Allies when

    (A) the United States broke off diplomatic relations with Germany
    (B) the United States entered the war on the Allied side
    (C) Italy joined the Allied side
    (D) Russia and Germany signed the Treaty of Brest-Litovsk
    (E) Japan annexed several German colonies in the Pacific

327. What was the significance of the Tannenberg campaign of 1914?

(A) It proved to the British that they could win the war on the seas.

(B) It demonstrated to the French that trench warfare would result only in a stalemate.

(C) It convinced the United States that the time had come to join the fight.

(D) It persuaded the Russians to rise up against the czar's government.

(E) It suggested to the Germans that they could win an easy victory on the Eastern Front.

328. World War I had all these devastating effects on Europe and its people EXCEPT

(A) it killed millions of soldiers and civilians

(B) it destroyed major cities and large towns

(C) it left tens of thousands of soldiers mentally ill from shellshock

(D) it laid waste to the countryside along the Western Front

(E) it ushered in an era of mechanized warfare

329. The United States emerged from the war as the world's strongest nation for all these reasons EXCEPT

(A) it was geographically far from the battle zones and therefore untouched

(B) it had lost relatively few troops in battle

(C) its economy received a boost from the war effort

(D) it played the leading role in the new League of Nations

(E) its efforts on the battlefield had strengthened its alliances with Britain and France

330. The victorious leaders redrew the map of Europe at Versailles in 1919 primarily in order to

(A) restore the balance of power and eliminate possible nationalist uprisings

(B) undo or reverse the 1871 unification of Germany

(C) create another large empire that would serve as a check on German aggressiveness

(D) prevent Russia from spreading Communism throughout Europe

(E) ensure that all the new states would be governed democratically

331. Which was NOT among the punitive measures forced on Germany at Versailles in 1919?

(A) It must return the territories of Alsace and Lorraine to France.
(B) It must permanently reduce its military to small defensive forces.
(C) It must admit sole and total responsibility for the war.
(D) It must work with Allied leaders to establish a new German government.
(E) It must pay large sums of money in compensation to the Allied nations.

332. The Balkan Wars of 1912–1913 resulted in all of the following EXCEPT

(A) the formation of the Balkan League
(B) the dismantling of Austrian influence in the Balkans
(C) the defeat of Bulgaria
(D) the alliance of Serbia with Greece and Romania
(E) major territorial gains for Serbia

Russia/Soviet Union from the 1905 Revolution to the Outbreak of World War II

333. Which factor did NOT contribute to the outbreak of the 1905 Revolution?

(A) the spread of Socialist, Communist, and liberal ideas
(B) the reactionary policies of the czar
(C) the emancipation of the serfs
(D) the effects of industrialization on the peasants
(E) the effects of a severe famine

334. The Russo-Japanese War was fought over the issue of

(A) Russia's eastward expansion
(B) Russia's naval assault on Japan
(C) Japan's invasion of eastern Russia
(D) Japan's refusal to trade with Russia
(E) Japan's imperialist goals in Southeast Asia

335. In the years between the 1905 Revolution and the buildup to World War I, Russia's foreign policy was governed by all of the following EXCEPT

(A) diplomatic agreements with France and Britain
(B) desire to recover its status as a formidable European power
(C) intent to expand its territory into the Balkans
(D) fear of German military and economic expansion
(E) reliance on the judgment of its experienced military officers

336. What was the outcome of the 1920 war between Poland and Russia?

(A) a Russian victory and an agreement on a permanent Russian-Polish border

(B) a Polish victory and an agreement on a permanent Russian-Polish border

(C) Russian military occupation of Poland

(D) Polish military occupation of Russia

(E) a Communist revolution in Poland

337. What was the result of the 1905 Revolution?

(A) The czar abdicated in favor of a temporary legislative assembly.

(B) The monarchy remained in authority by virtue of offering a compromise.

(C) The workers' councils seized control of the government.

(D) The nation descended into a long-lasting civil war among various factions.

(E) The military took over the government until elections could be held.

338. By carrying out the New Economic Policy of 1921, Lenin hoped to achieve all of the following EXCEPT

(A) to establish a mixed economy that included the best elements of Socialism and capitalism

(B) to reconcile the citizens to emergency measures taken by the government during the civil war

(C) to generate investment capital that could be pumped into industrialization

(D) to lay the foundation for Russia's transition to a full Socialist economy

(E) to stabilize production by establishing certain controls over the market

339. Which best describes the government that took power as a result of the February Revolution of 1917?

(A) an absolute dictator and his closest advisers

(B) a cabinet of chief ministers

(C) a group of high-ranking military officers

(D) a formal association of workers

(E) a liberal-to-centrist legislature

340. What was the result of the Russo-Japanese War?

(A) Russia gained access to the Sea of Japan.
(B) Russia annexed Japan.
(C) Russia made Japan a protectorate.
(D) Japan halted Russia's expansion into China.
(E) Japan acquired formerly Russian territory on the Asian mainland.

341. The Russian word *soviet* is best translated as

(A) Communist
(B) worker
(C) workers' council
(D) ministry
(E) province

342. The German invasion of Russia in 1914 had all the following effects on Russia EXCEPT

(A) it brought food shortages, famine, and starvation
(B) it extensively damaged the Russian railway system in the western part of the nation
(C) it abruptly halted Russian industrialization
(D) it showed that the Russian troops were better organized and stronger than the Germans
(E) it pulled thousands of men off the job and into military service

343. In 1917, Germany agreed to withdraw its troops from Russia in exchange for

(A) a significant amount of territory
(B) a mutual free-trade agreement
(C) financial compensation
(D) a Russian agreement never to attack Germany
(E) a promise of future Russian military aid if the need arose

344. The White Army in the Russian civil war of 1918–1921 was comprised of all the following groups EXCEPT

(A) royalists
(B) political moderates
(C) workers
(D) anti-Bolsheviks
(E) anti-Communists

345. Which is NOT one reason for the Red Army victory in the civil war?

(A) The Reds outnumbered the Whites.

(B) The Reds controlled Moscow and therefore the railroads.

(C) The Reds enjoyed widespread support among workers and peasants.

(D) The Reds had a clearly defined goal articulated by their leader, Lenin.

(E) The Reds had the support of important foreign allies.

346. Which best explains why the Bolsheviks failed in their goal of inciting similar revolutions throughout Europe?

(A) European Socialists had already achieved important concessions.

(B) Europeans were alarmed when they read of Lenin's brutal policies.

(C) Europeans considered Russia a barbaric, primitive nation.

(D) Europeans knew very little about the Bolshevik Revolution.

(E) Europeans were strongly opposed to Socialism as a political philosophy.

347. Which accurately describes Lenin's New Economic Policy?

(A) A new tax would be assessed in proportion to the income a person earned.

(B) The state would seize all private houses and make them into workers' apartments.

(C) The government would control wages of all urban factory workers.

(D) All formerly private property would in future belong to all the people collectively.

(E) The state would buy up all surplus crops for a fixed price in money or kind.

348. By boycotting the Versailles peace conference in 1919, Russia passed up a good chance to gain or regain

(A) formal international recognition of the new government

(B) some or all of the territory it had surrendered to Germany in 1918

(C) membership in the League of Nations

(D) the friendship of its World War I allies

(E) peace with Poland on favorable terms

349. The first Five-Year Plan, implemented in 1929, called for all of the following EXCEPT

(A) major public-works projects such as the building of the Moscow Metro

(B) the combining of many small farms into a few giant, state-run collectives

(C) the development of heavy industry

(D) the elimination of freedom of speech and of the press

(E) the employment of prison labor on large-scale construction projects

350. Which statement is NOT true of both the old czarist government of Russia and the new Communist government in the Soviet Union?

(A) The government had one absolute, autocratic ruler whose authority could not be questioned.

(B) The ruler embraced the Orthodox Church as the second major authority over the people.

(C) The head of the government did not tolerate political opposition in any form.

(D) The government regularly used the police and the military to put down popular opposition.

(E) There was no balance of powers in the government.

351. How did the Bolshevik Revolution differ from all previous European revolutions?

(A) It replaced one form of government with another.

(B) One of its major aims was to eliminate distinctions between social ranks.

(C) The new government could only be established at the cost of fighting a civil war.

(D) It was considered only the first step in overturning the existing social order throughout Europe.

(E) It resulted in the rise to power of a dictator whose authority could not be challenged.

352. Which is the most accurate description of the government of the newly organized Soviet Union in 1922?

(A) a one-party dictatorship

(B) a constitutional monarchy

(C) a parliamentary coalition government

(D) a democratic republic

(E) a workers' state

353. Which best describes the relationship between Stalin and the Soviet farmers?

    (A) Stalin worked to gain the farmers' wholehearted support.

    (B) Stalin despised the farmers and treated them almost as serfs.

    (C) Stalin respected the farmers more than any other group because they produced food.

    (D) Stalin paid no attention to the farmers.

    (E) Stalin denied the farmers all civil and political rights.

354. Lenin refused to create a Soviet legislature with any power or authority because he believed that parliaments were only the tools of

    (A) the artists and intellectuals

    (B) the agricultural workers

    (C) the urban workers

    (D) the merchants, business owners, and managers

    (E) the uneducated majority

The Rise of Totalitarianism in Europe and the Buildup to World War II

355. Which European nation or province came the closest to a successful Communist revolution in the wake of the Bolsheviks' rise to power in Russia?

    (A) Bavaria

    (B) Germany

    (C) Hungary

    (D) Slovakia

    (E) Spain

356. Which of the following is NOT one reason why Germany was able to defy the Versailles treaty and rearm with little opposition?

    (A) Other European nations were struggling with their own economic crises.

    (B) The fallout from the Great Depression discouraged all nations from foreign quarrels.

    (C) The European powers had agreed to suspend collection of German reparations.

    (D) The Allied occupation forces had been pulled out of the Rhineland.

    (E) Germany had stockpiled massive amounts of arms and ammunition during the 1920s.

357. As a result of the 1920 Treaty of Trianon, Hungary

    (A) lost more than half its territory and its people

    (B) received substantial financial reparations from Germany

    (C) agreed to maintain only a token army for defense in future

    (D) accepted the ruling authority of the League of Nations

    (E) recovered territory that had previously been annexed by Russia

358. Despite the rise of an authoritarian military regime in the late 1920s, all of the following continued to characterize Poland EXCEPT

    (A) the right to organize political parties

    (B) the right to form trade unions

    (C) freedom of religious worship

    (D) a free-market economy

    (E) relative freedom of the press, with very limited censorship

359. All these factors helped Fascism to succeed in Italy in 1920–1921 EXCEPT

    (A) division and disagreement between Socialist leaders and workers

    (B) the loss of Italian territory during the peace settlements at Versailles

    (C) government concessions to Socialist demands

    (D) a wave of widespread strikes, riots, and looting

    (E) soaring inflation and high unemployment

360. The strategy of autarky, adopted with varying success by a number of totalitarian states in the pre–World War II era, is defined as

    (A) political isolationism

    (B) one-party rule

    (C) censorship of the arts and the press

    (D) territorial imperialism

    (E) economic self-sufficiency

361. How did Hitler overcome disagreements between the radical and conservative wings of the Nazi Party in its first year of power?

    (A) He investigated which of the two would be more likely to keep the support of the German voters.

    (B) He had many of the radical leaders murdered by the SS (the Nazi Party's rogue militia).

    (C) He held a series of meetings in which the two sides worked out their differences.

    (D) He forced the radical Nazis to conform to the conservative platform.

    (E) He forced the conservative Nazis to conform to the radical platform.

362. Chancellor Engelbert Dollfuss imposed authoritarian rule on Austria in 1933 to stave off the perceived threat of

(A) the Nazis
(B) the Christian Socials
(C) the Social Democrats
(D) the German Nationalists
(E) the Catholic Church

363. Which factor did NOT contribute to the failure of Fascist rule in 1930s France?

(A) the lack of a single charismatic Fascist leader
(B) the strong French alliance with Britain
(C) the relative stability of the French economy
(D) the strong French tradition of republican government
(E) the lack of a perceived threat from the workers and the extreme political left

364. The young men who made up the committed core of the early Fascist squads in Italy were drawn from the ranks of all of the following EXCEPT

(A) World War I veterans
(B) civil servants
(C) middle-class merchants, shopkeepers, and small business owners
(D) daily wage laborers
(E) tenant farmers and small independent farmers

365. When Hitler first took power in 1933, Nazi Party members and sympathizers were generally agreed on all the following goals EXCEPT

(A) an end to domestic strife between social classes and political parties
(B) the severe suppression or elimination of Communism in Germany
(C) the elimination of religion in German society
(D) the recovery of Germany's status as a great European power
(E) a commitment to aggressive German nationalism

366. In the 1932 Treaty of Lausanne, the League of Nations granted Austria a substantial loan in exchange for

(A) the abandonment of plans for a customs union with Germany
(B) the granting of voting rights to all men age 21 and over
(C) the disbanding of the secret state police force
(D) the surrender of territory that historically belonged to Italy
(E) the granting of full independence to Hungary

367. The Spanish government that came to power in 1939 is best described as

(A) a democratic republic
(B) a workers' state
(C) a military dictatorship
(D) a constitutional monarchy
(E) an absolute monarchy

368. Which of the following pinpoints the major difference between the Nazi regime in Germany and the Fascist regime in Italy?

(A) Fascism was much less securely or unanimously established than Nazism.
(B) Fascism did not encourage territorial expansion as Nazism did.
(C) Unlike Nazism, Fascism was not a totalitarian form of government.
(D) Unlike Nazism, Fascism was not a government of one-party rule.
(E) Fascism did not result in tight censorship of the press as Nazism did.

369. All of the following are characteristic of the rise of a Communist state EXCEPT

(A) the use of propaganda that promotes Party ideology
(B) the crushing of any opposition party
(C) the support of the middle class
(D) Party control of all news media
(E) a violent overthrow of the previous government

370. In what way did the decisions of the leaders at Versailles in 1919 contribute to the success of the Nazi Party in Germany?

(A) by trying to punish Germany far more severely than was justified
(B) by excluding Germany from the peace conference
(C) by excluding Russia from the peace conference
(D) by allowing for future negotiation of the amount of the reparations
(E) by restoring the independence of Poland

371. Which of the following was most responsible for the European policy of appeasement toward Germany during the 1930s?

(A) Europeans did not know that Germany was rearming.
(B) Europeans believed that the United States was allied with Germany.
(C) Europeans supported an official union of Austria and Germany.
(D) Europeans overwhelmingly opposed war.
(E) Europeans did not object to Germany's annexation of Austria and Poland.

372. The Lateran Treaty of 1929 established mutual concessions between

(A) France and Germany
(B) the Soviet state and the Eastern Orthodox Church
(C) the Italian nation and the Catholic Church
(D) Austria and Hungary
(E) Germany and the Soviet Union

373. All of the following contributed to the rise of Fascism in the wake of World War I EXCEPT

(A) dissension among the parties representing the political left (the liberal side)
(B) the expansion of voting rights to include the uneducated classes
(C) the major role played in the war by a non-European nation (the United States)
(D) the enthusiasm of combat veterans for extreme nationalist rhetoric
(E) the combination of high unemployment and soaring inflation

374. France invaded the Ruhr in 1922 in order to

(A) seize in coal what Germany could not pay in money
(B) annex the region as French territory
(C) dissuade the Germans from a planned invasion of France
(D) aid the striking coal miners
(E) work with Germany to recover from the Great Depression

375. Why did the large landowners of northern Italy support the Fascists?

(A) Both were liberal.
(B) Both wanted to restore the monarchy.
(C) Both opposed the Socialists.
(D) Both were anti-Catholic.
(E) Both wanted war with Germany.

376. Why did the king of Italy fail to put down the Blackshirts when they marched into Rome in 1922?

(A) He wanted to avoid a full-scale civil war.
(B) He was afraid they would assassinate him.
(C) He did not command the loyalty of the Italian Army.
(D) He had made a secret pledge to Mussolini.
(E) He did not take their bluster seriously.

377. The Hitler Youth groups for boys and girls required all of the following EXCEPT

(A) regular participation in long country hikes
(B) paramilitary training (for boys only)
(C) political indoctrination
(D) manual labor and charity work
(E) a semester of study in a foreign country

378. During the 1930s, most high-ranking Spanish Catholics supported all of the following parties or individual leaders EXCEPT

(A) the Popular Front
(B) the National Front
(C) the Falange Party
(D) General Francisco Franco
(E) Miguel Primo de Rivera

379. Which Eastern European nation did NOT become a totalitarian state between 1919 and 1936?

(A) Czechoslovakia
(B) Hungary
(C) Poland
(D) Romania
(E) Yugoslavia

380. All successful European dictators of the post–World War I era depended on the personal loyalty of

(A) the press
(B) the armed forces
(C) the artists and intellectuals
(D) the civil service
(E) the common working people

381. Why did the Conservative Party in Britain oppose Prime Minister Ramsay MacDonald?

(A) He extended unemployment benefits.
(B) He spoke out in favor of universal free public education.
(C) He reestablished trade relations with Germany.
(D) He extended both loans and diplomatic recognition to the USSR.
(E) He persuaded the Trades Union Congress to end a national workers' strike.

382. What was the guiding principle behind the policies of the French government between the world wars?

(A) to protect itself against future German aggression
(B) to reestablish its economy on a sound footing
(C) to pass major social reforms
(D) to prepare its African and Asian colonies for self-government
(E) to resume foreign trade

383. The Weimar Republic was famous for bold experimentation in the arts, including works by all of the following EXCEPT

(A) Bertolt Brecht
(B) George Grosz
(C) Joseph von Sternberg
(D) Igor Stravinsky
(E) Kurt Weill

384. The inability of the liberal, constitutional German politicians to agree on their goals during the 1920s led to all of the following EXCEPT

(A) a sharp rise in extreme German nationalism
(B) loss of the people's confidence in and support for their leaders
(C) deep-seated bitterness over the defeat in World War I
(D) defeat in a series of negotiations over Versailles Treaty provisions
(E) a series of more than a dozen coalition governments in 14 years

385. Which of the following came to power in the 1936 national elections in Spain?

(A) the Communist Party
(B) the Falange Party
(C) the Fascist Party
(D) the National Front
(E) the Popular Front

386. In his dramatic rise to power, Hitler employed all the following tactics to win the support of the German voters EXCEPT

(A) describing specific steps he would take to end unemployment
(B) bullying and intimidating his political opponents
(C) continually referring to Germany's history as a great power
(D) constantly repeating simple, easily memorized political slogans
(E) deliberately appealing to the emotions and prejudices of the common people

387. Which statement is NOT true of both Mussolini and Hitler?

(A) Each was a World War I combat veteran.

(B) Each was an absolute dictator in a one-party government.

(C) Each employed brutal, bullying tactics against the opposition.

(D) Each had been a failure in civilian life before rising to political power.

(E) Each pursued an aggressive, expansion-minded foreign policy.

388. Why did the established German political parties fail to take Hitler seriously when he first appeared on the scene in the late 1920s?

(A) He could not communicate effectively with the common people.

(B) He had no experience of government or politics.

(C) He spoke enthusiastically about a German empire that had never really existed.

(D) His only followers were unemployed World War I combat veterans.

(E) He was Austrian rather than German by birth.

389. All of the following are true of both Communism and Fascism as practiced in 20th-century Europe EXCEPT

(A) both instituted one-party rule

(B) both rigidly censored the press and the arts

(C) both encouraged extreme, excessive nationalism in the people

(D) both inevitably led to serious economic collapse

(E) both used the army and police as instruments of fear to control the people

390. Which of the following was NOT an immediate and direct result of Hitler's rise to power?

(A) As many as one-fourth of all German Jews left the country.

(B) Thousands of German artists and intellectuals emigrated.

(C) One-party (Nazi) rule became the law of the land.

(D) The German economy recovered from its 1922 collapse.

(E) A secret state police force, the Gestapo, was created to carry out Hitler's direct orders.

World War II

391. The Axis Powers had the upper hand on the battlefield for the first three years of the war for all of the following reasons EXCEPT

(A) as the aggressor or challenger nations, they were able to control the course of events

(B) they had laid careful plans for the war, unlike the Allied Powers

(C) their troops outnumbered the Allied troops

(D) the German army was extremely well-disciplined

(E) almost all the nations of Europe were under Axis control

392. Which was NOT one provision of the Potsdam Conference of 1945?

(A) Austria and Germany would be occupied by the victorious Allied forces, with each Allied nation controlling its own zone.

(B) Poland would retain German territory it had taken during the war.

(C) Germany would pay reparations to all the Allied nations.

(D) Germany would pay the greatest amount of reparations to the Allied nation that had suffered the greatest losses.

(E) Only the United States would occupy Japan after the war ended.

393. Why did the Soviet Union join the Allied nations in 1941?

(A) because Japan attacked the United States

(B) because the United States entered the war on the Allied side

(C) because Germany invaded the Soviet Union

(D) because Germany annexed Austria

(E) because Italy entered the war on the Axis side

394. In which region did the U.S. Army first go into battle against the Axis Powers?

(A) on the Soviet border

(B) in northern France

(C) in central Germany

(D) in the Balkans

(E) in North Africa

395. Which nation was by far the greatest sufferer at the end of the war, in terms of lives lost?

(A) Britain

(B) France

(C) Germany

(D) Italy

(E) the Soviet Union

396. The Allied invasion of Normandy in 1944 was a success because the Germans

(A) had expected the invasion to take place in a different location
(B) had sent too many divisions east to fight the Soviets
(C) could not decipher the Allied coded messages
(D) already knew that they were bound to lose the war
(E) did not believe the Allied generals could plan a successful invasion

397. Hitler was eager to recover the Danzig Corridor from Poland because

(A) it would provide Germany with a port on the Baltic Sea
(B) it was rich in minerals and other natural resources
(C) he intended it to be a buffer zone between Germany and Poland
(D) it would protect Germany from possible overland attack by the USSR
(E) it physically separated East Prussia from the rest of Germany

398. Which best describes the Vichy regime (1940–1944)?

(A) a right-wing French government under the sway of Nazi authority
(B) a bureaucracy staffed and run by Nazi officers stationed throughout France
(C) an armed, underground movement of popular resistance to Nazi authority in France
(D) a French Communist government collaborating with Stalin and the Soviets
(E) a German army of occupation carrying out French domestic policy

399. The Maginot Line was a series of defensive fortifications built along

(A) the border between Poland and the Soviet Union
(B) the border between France and Germany
(C) the southern coast of England
(D) the border between France and Spain
(E) the border between Italy and Austria

400. One reason Hitler underestimated the abilities of the Soviet troops was his mistaken belief that

(A) the Soviet Union was not that large a nation
(B) Soviets were racially inferior to Germans
(C) the Soviet troops would not prove loyal to Stalin
(D) Britain and France would not welcome the Soviets as allies
(E) the Soviet Union had a powerful navy

401. Which best describes Hitler's original ambition in the years before World War II?

    (A) to make Germany a military and economic superpower

    (B) to subdue and control Britain and France

    (C) to exterminate the Jews and Slavs of Eastern Europe

    (D) to form a lasting alliance with the Soviet Union

    (E) to conquer Europe by means of fighting an all-out, two-front war

402. All of the following were important activities of the French Resistance EXCEPT

    (A) publishing uncensored news of the war

    (B) organizing escape routes out of France for Allied pilots and soldiers

    (C) spying on the occupying German officials and the French collaborators

    (D) carrying out sabotage in the munitions industry

    (E) operating a profitable black market

403. The term *D-Day* refers to which of the following?

    (A) the appointment of Winston Churchill as prime minister of Britain (May 10, 1939)

    (B) the German invasion of the Soviet Union (June 22, 1940)

    (C) the Japanese bombing of Pearl Harbor, Hawaii (December 7, 1941)

    (D) the Allied invasion of Normandy in northern France (June 6, 1944)

    (E) the liberation of Paris by the Allies (August 25, 1944)

404. Which of the following was NOT a major victory for the Allied side?

    (A) the siege of Stalingrad

    (B) the Battle of El Alamein

    (C) the Battle of the Bulge

    (D) the retreat at Dunkirk

    (E) the invasion of Normandy

405. Before war was formally declared in September 1939, Nazi Germany had already invaded and subdued all of the following EXCEPT

    (A) Austria

    (B) Czechoslovakia

    (C) France

    (D) Poland

    (E) the Rhineland

406. Which of the European powers was NOT represented at the Munich peace conference of 1938?

(A) Britain
(B) France
(C) Germany
(D) Italy
(E) the Soviet Union

407. Which best describes France's role in World War II between June 1940 and August 1944?

(A) a fully committed fighter on the Allied side of the war
(B) a fully committed fighter on the Axis side of the war
(C) an occupied nation under the sway of Nazi Germany
(D) a nation fully taken up in a desperate civil war
(E) a neutral nation whose sympathies were with the Allied side

408. All these factors contributed substantially to the German defeat on the Eastern Front EXCEPT

(A) great geographical distance between the German troops and their source of supply
(B) the fierceness and tenacity of the Soviet troops in defense and counterattack
(C) heavy German losses in both troops and equipment
(D) disloyalty to Hitler among the German military command
(E) German inability to cope with the Russian climate, especially in the winter of 1941–1942

409. Hitler's serious strategic errors of judgment made during World War II include all of the following EXCEPT

(A) the two-pronged attack on France in the spring of 1940
(B) the declaration of war against the United States in the wake of Pearl Harbor
(C) the abandonment of the nonaggression pact with the Soviet Union
(D) the annexation of several Eastern European states into the German Reich
(E) the belief that the British and French guarantee of Polish sovereignty was a bluff

410. When the Allied armies invaded the Italian mainland in 1943,
  (A) Mussolini committed suicide to avoid being tried as a war criminal
  (B) German troops abandoned the fight in North Africa to come to Italy's rescue
  (C) the king of Italy appointed a new prime minister and signed an armistice with the Allies
  (D) Hitler denounced the Italians as cowards and immediately broke off the Italo-German alliance
  (E) the Allied commanders immediately began organizing the restructure of the Italian government

411. The term *Battle of Britain* refers to
  (A) the Allied bombing of German cities
  (B) the decision of the British royal family and the prime minister to remain in London in spite of the danger of the bombing
  (C) the British retreat across the English Channel in the wake of the German invasion of France
  (D) the British naval blockade of the German ships in the North Sea
  (E) the German bombing of British cities

412. Which does NOT describe one way in which war conditions affected civilian populations throughout Europe?
  (A) The government rationed ordinary consumer goods such as food, cigarettes, and clothing.
  (B) Unemployment was high and jobs, apart from military service, were scarce.
  (C) People were in constant danger of being killed by stray bombs or bullets or by deliberate acts of violence.
  (D) Families were separated because parents sent their children to safe areas away from military targets.
  (E) The Nazis encouraged ordinary people to watch and report on one another's activities.

413. In the fall of 1938, the leaders of Europe agreed to partition
  (A) Austria
  (B) Czechoslovakia
  (C) France
  (D) Poland
  (E) the Soviet Union

414. European military commanders found that a relentless air attack on the enemy, particularly in areas populated by civilians, was highly effective for all these reasons EXCEPT

(A) it was a divisive force among the civilians because it maintained a high level of fear
(B) it destroyed crucial infrastructure such as railroads
(C) it regularly prevented civilians from going to work, which in turn hampered productivity
(D) it forced the enemy to use up valuable equipment and resources in defense against it
(E) it caused civilians to lose confidence in the government because the government was helpless to protect them against it

415. Which best describes the conspirators who attempted to assassinate Hitler in the summer of 1944?

(A) Allied military officers
(B) conservative Germans of high social rank
(C) the French Resistance
(D) ordinary German people
(E) highly placed SS and Gestapo officials

416. What became of the nation of Austria as a result of the *Anschluss*?

(A) It was ruled by a puppet Austrian government subordinate to the Nazis.
(B) It was considered part of a newly enlarged Germany and was ruled directly from Berlin.
(C) It was granted protectorate status as a German satellite state.
(D) It was occupied by the Nazis and placed under military rule for the duration of the war.
(E) It was granted equal status with Germany as Hitler's homeland and a culturally and linguistically German nation.

417. Which was NOT a factor in Hitler's decision to take the serious risk of invading the Soviet Union?

(A) He despised Communism on ideological grounds and wanted to stamp it out.
(B) He wanted to expand Germany's territory into Soviet lands.
(C) He sensed that Stalin had territorial ambitions in Eastern Europe that would conflict with German imperialism.
(D) He believed that the Soviets were weak and would be defeated easily.
(E) He knew that invading the Soviet Union was a necessary first step toward conquering China.

418. What was the overriding factor in the U.S. decision to fight in the defense of Western Europe first, instead of sending troops to the Eastern Front to aid the Soviet Union?

(A) economics
(B) politics
(C) geography
(D) sentiment
(E) loyalty

419. The phrase "peace in our time" refers to an agreement made by the leaders of the European powers at

(A) Munich in 1938
(B) Paris in 1940
(C) Rome in 1943
(D) Yalta in 1945
(E) Potsdam in 1945

420. All of the following European nations remained officially neutral during World War II EXCEPT

(A) Norway
(B) Spain
(C) Sweden
(D) Switzerland
(E) Turkey

421. From the late 1930s into 1940, Mussolini attempted to expand Italy's sphere of influence into

(A) the large Mediterranean islands
(B) Austria and Poland
(C) France and Spain
(D) North Africa and the Balkans
(E) Scandinavia

422. Germany was able to invade France with relative ease because

(A) the Maginot Line did not block a German invasion
(B) the French had taken no precautions against German aggression
(C) France had no air force or navy to compare to those of Germany
(D) there were deep political divisions within the French leadership
(E) Britain refused to come to the aid of the French troops

423. What was Stalin's main motive for the 1939 pact he signed with Hitler?

    (A) to avoid having to fight a two-front war against the Allies

    (B) to acquire territory in Poland and on the Baltic

    (C) to protect Soviet supremacy over the small states of Eastern Europe

    (D) to eliminate any possibility of Soviet involvement in a European war

    (E) to ally the Soviet Union with another large Communist nation

424. At the Yalta Conference, Stalin promised Roosevelt that as soon as the war in Europe was won, he would

    (A) lead Soviet troops into Berlin

    (B) establish Communism throughout Eastern Europe

    (C) abolish Communism in the Soviet Union

    (D) accept Soviet membership in the United Nations

    (E) send Soviet troops to the Pacific to support the United States in the fight against Japan

425. Between the beginning of the European war in 1939 and its own entry into the war in 1941, the United States took all these steps to aid the Allies EXCEPT

    (A) establishing a lend-lease program with Britain

    (B) funding the Manhattan Project

    (C) selling surplus goods to Britain and France

    (D) establishing diplomatic relations with the Soviet Union

    (E) sending troops to Europe for training and special missions

426. Which does NOT describe one result of the 1939 Nazi and Soviet invasions of Poland?

    (A) All Polish territory was annexed by Germany and the USSR.

    (B) Both Nazis and Soviets established total state control over the Polish economy.

    (C) Religious worship was outlawed throughout Poland.

    (D) Tens of thousands of Poles were imprisoned, deported, or virtually enslaved.

    (E) Both Nazis and Soviets cracked down on Polish culture, including the use of the Polish language.

427. Although Franco refused to join either the Axis or the Allied side, Spain participated in World War II in all these ways EXCEPT

(A) joining in the Allied invasion of Normandy in 1944

(B) sending Spanish troops to the Eastern Front to support Germany's invasion of the Soviet Union

(C) permitting refugees bound for Portugal to travel freely through Spain

(D) issuing Spanish passports to Jewish refugees to help them escape Europe

(E) supplying the German munitions industry with essential metals

CHAPTER 5

The Cold War and the Fall of Communism

The Cold War and the Dismantling of European Empires to 1968

428. What was the result of Britain's withdrawal from India in 1947?

(A) India became a hereditary monarchy.
(B) India became two independent states, India and Pakistan.
(C) Communist China invaded India.
(D) India severed all diplomatic and trade relations with Britain.
(E) India and Pakistan began to work on a plan of union.

429. Stalin determined to establish a safety zone of Soviet satellite nations on the USSR's western border after World War II mainly because of his recent memories of

(A) nuclear bombings
(B) economic collapse
(C) German invasions of the USSR
(D) czarist rule under the old regime
(E) peace conferences

430. Of all the African nations that achieved independence in the post–World War II era, those that had been colonized by Britain achieved it the most smoothly because

(A) Britain's former colonies boasted greater natural resources
(B) Britain's former colonies were larger and more populous
(C) Britain's former colonies had a higher percentage of educated Africans with administrative experience
(D) Britain maintained closer connections with its former African colonies
(E) Britain ensured a peaceful transfer of power in each of its former African colonies

431. All of the following consequences of World War II contributed significantly to the swift rise of Communist rule in Eastern Europe EXCEPT

(A) enormous loss of professionals, intellectuals, and merchants (due to death or emigration) that opened up opportunities for others to take their places

(B) the often brutal behavior of the Soviet troops on the march through Eastern Europe toward Berlin

(C) improvement in industrial production due to being forced to supply the Nazis throughout the war

(D) wartime increase in the government's hands-on control of various businesses and industries

(E) the wartime breakdown of normal social and class ranks and social institutions

432. One advantage of life under Communist rule in Eastern Europe was

(A) freedom of artistic expression

(B) comfortable housing

(C) universal employment

(D) full social equality

(E) high wages

433. Communist Party candidates went through all the following steps to take over the nations of Eastern Europe after 1945 EXCEPT

(A) temporarily forming coalitions with other political parties

(B) gaining individual positions of influence in the bureaucracy, police, and armed forces

(C) carrying out campaigns of brutal intimidation against all political opponents

(D) acquiring a political base by pretending that they were not Communists

(E) imposing totalitarian rule and banning all non-Communist political parties

434. The 1956 uprising in Poland resulted in

(A) a major Soviet military crackdown

(B) the overthrow of the Communist Party

(C) the return of the long-exiled Polish government from London

(D) massive defections to Western Europe

(E) Wladyslaw Gomulka's rise to the leadership of the nation

435. Why did the East Germans build the Berlin Wall?

   (A) to prevent Westerners from crossing freely into East Berlin
   (B) to prevent East Germans from crossing freely into West Berlin
   (C) to prevent violent civil war from breaking out in Berlin
   (D) to block official Allied access into East Berlin
   (E) to put an end to any friendly contact between citizens of West and East Berlin

436. During which occasion did a threat from the Soviet Union come closest to causing a nuclear war between it and the United States?

   (A) the Korean War
   (B) the Vietnam War
   (C) the blockade of West Berlin
   (D) the Bay of Pigs invasion
   (E) the Cuban Missile Crisis

437. The term *Prague Spring* refers to which event in Czechoslovakia's history?

   (A) the establishment of the new state of Czechoslovakia as a democratic republic in 1919
   (B) the establishment of an independent Socialist government under Eduard Benes in 1945
   (C) the replacement of Eduard Benes with Communist leader Klement Gottwald in 1948
   (D) the sweeping liberal reforms instituted by Alexander Dubcek in 1968
   (E) the breakup of Czechoslovakia into two independent republics in 1993

438. Which Eastern European nation successfully resisted Soviet control in the wake of World War II?

   (A) Czechoslovakia
   (B) Hungary
   (C) Poland
   (D) Romania
   (E) Yugoslavia

439. When Germany surrendered in 1945, which Allied nation did NOT install an army of occupation in Berlin?

   (A) Britain
   (B) France
   (C) Italy
   (D) the Soviet Union
   (E) the United States

440. What was the result of U.S. and Soviet intervention into the former Belgian colony of the Congo?

(A) Patrice Lumumba was assassinated and a Congolese civil war broke out soon after.

(B) Belgian troops of occupation withdrew from the Congo.

(C) United Nations officials supervised democratic elections in the Congo.

(D) Belgium granted protectorate status to the Congo with United Nations approval.

(E) The Congo broke up into two independent states along ethnic and tribal lines.

441. Which of the following was among the major motives for the Allied occupation of Germany and Berlin in 1945?

(A) to help the Germans rearm and reorganize their military forces

(B) to include the German leaders in plans being made for the United Nations

(C) to humiliate and punish Germany in retaliation for its aggression under Hitler

(D) to divide Germany into two independent, self-governing nations

(E) to wipe out all remaining elements of Nazism and the Nazi Party

442. Winston Churchill coined the term *Iron Curtain* to refer to

(A) the western border of the Soviet Union

(B) the Berlin Wall

(C) the border between Western Europe and Communist Eastern Europe

(D) the border between North and South Vietnam

(E) the border between Communist China and the Soviet Union

443. When World War II ended, the leaders of Italy were faced with all these serious internal questions EXCEPT

(A) what the Catholic Church's role in Italian society would be

(B) whether and how to punish former Fascist officials

(C) what type of representative government to adopt

(D) what provisions should be written into a new constitution

(E) how to resolve the immediate postwar economic crisis

444. The post–World War II decades in Western Europe are best characterized as an era of

(A) economic hardship
(B) international cooperation
(C) massive defense spending
(D) political reform
(E) political conservatism

445. The United States developed the Marshall Plan in order to offer financial aid to

(A) all the Communist nations of Europe
(B) all the freely elected republics of Europe
(C) all nations that had fought on the Allied side in the war
(D) all the nations of Europe
(E) all the nations that had fought in the war on either side

446. Which best describes the provisions of the North Atlantic Treaty Organization (NATO), formed in 1949?

(A) Each member nation would treat an attack on any of the others as an attack on itself.
(B) Member nations would pool their economic resources to rebuild Europe.
(C) Member nations would establish a common arsenal of atomic weapons for their mutual defense if necessary.
(D) Member nations would support insurrection against oppression anywhere it arose in the world.
(E) Member nations would trade freely with one another, eliminating all tariffs and other trade barriers.

447. Which is NOT one consequence of the Twentieth Party Congress held in the USSR in 1956?

(A) Tens of thousands of Soviet prisoners were released from the gulags.
(B) Non-Communist candidates were allowed to run for political office at the local level.
(C) Eastern Europeans were encouraged to test the strength of the post-Stalinist Soviet government by rebelling against it.
(D) The state denounced many of Stalin's worst excesses, thus informing most Soviets of them for the first time.
(E) Conflict and rioting broke out during the process of repatriation of foreign prisoners.

448. During the peace process and the occupation of Berlin in 1945, Stalin's distrust of his allies was largely based on

(A) their attempt to share the credit when the Soviet Army took Berlin
(B) their desire to create an international peacekeeping organization
(C) his inability to understand their statements without an interpreter
(D) his conviction that they intended to impose a capitalist economy on Germany
(E) his resentment over the undue burden the Soviets had borne on the battlefield

449. When the governments of Czechoslovakia and Hungary passed sweeping economic reforms during the Cold War, the Soviet Union responded by

(A) agreeing to study the effect of the new programs on the national economies
(B) sending troops into both nations to restore the status quo
(C) executing the leaders who instituted the reforms and replacing them with Soviet puppets
(D) instituting similar reforms in other Soviet-controlled Communist states
(E) disbanding the legislatures in both states and calling for new elections

450. The Berlin Airlift accomplished which of the following?

(A) defended West Berlin from a planned East German air attack
(B) helped Jewish refugees in Berlin make their way to Israel
(C) made it possible for East Germans to flee to the West
(D) helped German refugees to return to their homes
(E) delivered food and supplies into West Berlin in spite of a blockade

451. After Stalin's death, Soviet premier Nikita Khrushchev instituted all the following steps toward reform in the Soviet Union EXCEPT

(A) the state began investing more in agricultural production
(B) the bureaucracy was decentralized, giving more authority to the republics
(C) censorship of the press and the arts was relaxed (not eliminated)
(D) the state ceased to speak of or treat Stalin as a great national hero
(E) a series of major peace talks with the United States began

452. During the Cold War, it became clear that the great powers of Western Europe

(A) had been turned into satellites of the United States
(B) had developed into superpowers
(C) had fallen under Communist control
(D) had dwindled into minor or secondary powers
(E) had lost their belief in popularly elected representative government

453. Which European nation was NOT on the Soviet-controlled side of the Iron Curtain?

(A) Austria
(B) East Germany
(C) Hungary
(D) Poland
(E) Romania

454. Leaders on both sides of the Cold War supported the partition of Germany into two independent nations because

(A) they believed that Germany's economic and military status was the key to the strength of Europe as a whole
(B) they were afraid that a weak or neutral Germany might swing the balance in the Cold War to the enemy side
(C) they were afraid that a strong, united Germany might once again threaten world peace and security
(D) they could not forgive Germany for having caused two major wars of aggression within 50 years
(E) they were secretly afraid that the forces of Nazism would rise again despite the defeat of 1945

455. Which issue was the root cause of the armed conflict that broke out in Dutch-controlled Indonesia and French-controlled Indochina in 1948–1949?

(A) Communism
(B) nationalism
(C) economics
(D) conservatism
(E) national security

456. During the Cold War, Western Europeans enjoyed all of the following EXCEPT

(A) unprecedented choices in consumer goods
(B) improvement in the types and quality of food available
(C) freedom from fear of totalitarianism
(D) plentiful job opportunities
(E) a sharp rise in individual income

457. As World War II drew to a close, Soviet goals for the immediate future included all of the following EXCEPT

(A) to avoid an outbreak of hostility with Western allies, particularly the United States and Britain
(B) to eliminate forever the threat of German aggression or invasion
(C) to gain international respect and recognition as a great power
(D) to secure Western acceptance of plans for Soviet expansion to prewar borders
(E) to support strong, Soviet-friendly, independent governments throughout Eastern Europe

458. When the Cold War began, the United States had all these advantages over the Soviet Union EXCEPT

(A) a more prosperous economy
(B) a larger population
(C) a far lower casualty total from World War II
(D) no physical damage to its land or cities
(E) greater military strength

459. Which is NOT one major reform that took place in Poland during the late 1950s?

(A) a return to partial power and influence of the Church in Poland
(B) the end to one-party Communist rule
(C) the dissolution of the large collective farms
(D) easing of the regulations governing travel abroad for Poles
(E) improvements in trade agreements with the USSR

460. Which of the following was established after World War II as an international peacekeeping organization?

(A) the League of Nations
(B) the North Atlantic Treaty Organization
(C) the Quadruple Alliance
(D) the United Nations
(E) the Warsaw Pact

461. During the 1950s, the most common method of protest against Communist rule in East Germany was

(A) to emigrate westward
(B) to join the underground armed resistance movement
(C) to go on strike
(D) to publish articles in the press
(E) to riot in the streets

462. Which of the following did NOT contribute significantly to Nikita Khrushchev's fall from power in the mid-1960s?

(A) the Berlin Crisis of 1961 and the Cuban Missile Crisis of 1962
(B) overspending on foreign aid to India and other nations
(C) the emphasis on de-Stalinization
(D) persecution campaigns against prominent writers and artists
(E) the failure of ill-conceived agricultural policies

463. The Marshall Plan aid was intended, over the long term, to enable European nations to achieve all of the following EXCEPT

(A) to lower tariffs and thus increase international trade
(B) to achieve economic self-sufficiency
(C) to stabilize national currencies
(D) to increase manufacturing and industry
(E) to pursue sound economic policies

464. What decision did the Italian government reach about the surviving Fascists after World War II?

(A) It took away their Italian citizenship.
(B) It put them on trial for war crimes.
(C) It issued a general amnesty.
(D) It banned them from holding any government office in the future.
(E) It fined them heavily.

465. Which of the following was NOT a major aspect of West German policy under Chancellor Konrad Adenauer during the 1950s?

(A) friendship with the United States
(B) economic and political integration into the Western European community
(C) forming an alliance with Poland
(D) becoming a member of NATO
(E) refusing to recognize the state of East Germany

The Fall of Communism to 1991

466. The Congress of People's Deputies, created in the USSR in 1988, is best described as

(A) a genuine representative legislature
(B) a body of electors who would choose the Supreme Soviet
(C) a special council to the president of the Soviet Republic of Russia
(D) a cabinet of chief ministers to the executive
(E) a committee to plan the formal dissolution of the Soviet Union

467. Which was NOT one form of popular resistance to Communist rule behind the Iron Curtain?

(A) Political activists led armed uprisings against the government.
(B) Writers smuggled their works into the West for publication.
(C) Prominent individuals defected to Western nations.
(D) Communist leaders were assassinated.
(E) Workers fought for collective bargaining rights.

468. Uprisings and protest movements throughout Italy from about 1968 to 1973 had all these goals EXCEPT

(A) greater government controls
(B) a better system of higher education
(C) greater job opportunities for educated youths
(D) higher wages and greater benefits for workers
(E) women's rights

469. During the Prague Spring of 1968, Alexander Dubcek supported or instituted all the following reforms EXCEPT

(A) allowing non-Communist candidates to run for office
(B) encouraging freedom of expression on political topics
(C) investigating Stalinist purges of the 1950s
(D) the creation of a federated Czech-Slovak state
(E) accountability of the leadership to the citizens

470. Which nation broke into two independent republics soon after the end of the Cold War?

(A) Austria
(B) Czechoslovakia
(C) Greece
(D) Poland
(E) Romania

471. All of the following contributed significantly to the downfall of Communism in Poland from about 1978 to 1980 EXCEPT

(A) the Catholic Church
(B) scholars and intellectuals
(C) factory workers
(D) bureaucrats
(E) political dissenters

472. The major goals of the Conference on Security and Cooperation in Europe, held from 1973 to 1975, included all of the following EXCEPT

(A) the lifting of most international travel restrictions within Europe
(B) mutual recognition of the current European borders
(C) official acceptance of the permanent division of Germany
(D) a fundamental commitment to basic individual human freedoms
(E) the easing of trade across the Iron Curtain in both directions

473. Which was NOT one result or consequence of the May 1968 movement in France?

(A) The government raised the national minimum wage.
(B) The government called for new elections.
(C) Liberal movements such as environmentalism and feminism began to cohere.
(D) The right wing in French politics gained a massive majority in the legislature.
(E) President Charles de Gaulle resigned from office.

474. In the years immediately following the death of Stalin, the Soviet government became

(A) substantially more democratic
(B) more centralized and bureaucratic
(C) somewhat less repressive
(D) substantially harsher and more repressive
(E) smaller and more streamlined

475. What was the result of Mikhail Gorbachev's policy of *glasnost* in the USSR?

(A) Special privileges for Party members were eliminated.
(B) Non-Communists were permitted to run for office.
(C) The USSR and the United States began discussing nuclear disarmament.
(D) The Communist Party split into moderate and radical factions.
(E) A plurality of political views and opinions were openly expressed.

476. The Commonwealth of Independent States (the successor to the USSR) links the member nations for all the following purposes EXCEPT

(A) military defense and security
(B) international financial policy
(C) local administration
(D) the administration of justice
(E) internal and external trade regulations

477. Which of the following best describes Solidarity of Poland?

(A) an underground free press
(B) a Communist Party organization
(C) a dock workers' union
(D) an armed underground resistance movement
(E) a powerful political party

478. Which of the following events brought the Berlin Wall down in less than 24 hours?

(A) a speech by U.S. President Ronald Reagan
(B) an official visit to East Berlin by Mikhail Gorbachev
(C) an East German official's misstatement to the press
(D) the Velvet Revolution in Czechoslovakia
(E) the order for the opening of the Iron Curtain between Hungary and Austria

479. Which of the following was never a member of the Commonwealth of Independent States?

(A) Armenia
(B) the Baltic republics (Estonia, Latvia, Lithuania)
(C) Georgia
(D) Russia
(E) the Ukraine

480. The European Economic Community, later called the European Union, was founded as a result of a 1950 agreement between

(A) Britain and France
(B) France and Germany
(C) Germany and Austria
(D) Austria and France
(E) Germany and Britain

481. Into which nation did the Soviet Union send troops in 1979 to support the Communist government, with disastrous consequences to itself?

(A) Afghanistan
(B) Czechoslovakia
(C) Egypt
(D) Israel
(E) Yugoslavia

482. The political concept of *perestroika* is best defined as

(A) an agreement between nations to exist peacefully side by side
(B) a restructuring of government and society
(C) a receptiveness to political opinions from all social ranks
(D) the absolute right of the majority party to rule the state
(E) the elimination of tariffs between international trading partners

483. Lech Walesa of Poland is a notable figure in history for all these reasons EXCEPT

(A) winning the Nobel Peace Prize
(B) organizing an international workers' union throughout Eastern Europe
(C) becoming the first democratically elected president of Poland since World War II
(D) leading the political opposition against Poland's Communist government in the 1980s
(E) leading the workers' strikes and the movement that became Solidarity

484. In 1989–1990, civil war broke out in Yugoslavia over the issue of

(A) economics
(B) resistance to Communist rule
(C) censorship of the press
(D) nationalism
(E) foreign policy

485. Which does NOT characterize changes in the Soviet dissident movement from the 1960s to the 1970s?

(A) It became much more political.
(B) Thousands more people participated.
(C) It gained major concessions from the government.
(D) Many ethnic minorities joined the movement.
(E) The movement was better organized.

486. In 1988–1989, all of the following contributed substantially to the rise of democratic rule in Poland EXCEPT

(A) the government's failed attempt to impose martial law on the nation

(B) the Soviet announcement that it considered Poland a fully independent nation

(C) a wave of workers' strikes throughout the nation

(D) the government's invitation to the opposition to participate in talks about the economic crisis

(E) the overwhelming defeat of the Communists in the elections of June 1989

487. What type of government succeeded the authoritarian regime of Francisco Franco in Spain?

(A) a democratic republic

(B) a Communist state

(C) a military dictatorship

(D) an absolute monarchy

(E) a constitutional monarchy

488. Which was NOT one aspect of West German Chancellor Willy Brandt's policy of *Ostpolitik*, announced on his rise to power in 1969?

(A) a pledge to sign the nuclear Nonproliferation Treaty

(B) official recognition of East Germany as a sovereign state

(C) support for a nonaggression agreement with East Germany

(D) peaceful outreach toward Czechoslovakia and Poland

(E) support for a settlement with East Germany over the status of Berlin

489. Great Britain in the 1970s and 1980s under Prime Minister Margaret Thatcher was characterized by all of the following EXCEPT

(A) a drop in economic growth

(B) soaring unemployment

(C) rioting in the old manufacturing centers

(D) a sharp drop in trade-union membership

(E) higher taxes

490. All of the following were instrumental in ending Communism in Poland EXCEPT

(A) the election of Cardinal Karol Józef Wojtyla as Pope John Paul II

(B) the awarding of the Nobel Prize for literature to Czeslaw Milosz

(C) the appointment of General Wojciech Jaruzelski as prime minister

(D) the government's concession to the workers' demands to unionize

(E) the formation of Solidarity under the leadership of Lech Walesa

491. The Charter 77 Movement that arose in Czechoslovakia in the mid-1970s demanded

(A) that the citizens rise up against the government
(B) that workers throughout the nation go on strike
(C) that the government hold free elections
(D) that the government sever its ties to the USSR
(E) that the government obey its own laws

492. Which was NOT one reason why Soviet leader Leonid Brezhnev pursued a policy of *détente* with the United States in the 1970s?

(A) He hoped to gain American support for a settlement of the Vietnam War.
(B) He wanted the United States to extend diplomatic recognition to East Germany.
(C) He hoped to ease trade relations between the superpowers.
(D) He hoped to balance hostile relations with China against friendlier relations with the United States.
(E) He wanted the Soviet Union to benefit from American technology.

493. What steps did the Italian government take to quell the protest movement that began around 1968?

(A) It substantially raised industrial wages.
(B) It cracked down on corruption in the government.
(C) It legalized divorce.
(D) It reformed pension and tax laws to benefit the workers.
(E) It instituted a long-promised system of regional government.

494. The May 1968 movement in France is best characterized as

(A) a nationwide call for Algerian independence
(B) a left-wing uprising calling for a revolution in government
(C) a shift in government powers from the president toward the legislature
(D) a shift in government powers from the legislature toward the president
(E) nationwide opposition to national policy toward West Germany

495. Josip Broz Tito of Yugoslavia is historically significant for all these reasons EXCEPT

(A) being the most successful resistance leader in Europe during World War II

(B) refusing to tolerate Soviet interference in the affairs of Yugoslavia

(C) being expelled from the Comintern despite his commitment to Socialism

(D) winning the Nobel Prize for his efforts toward international peace

(E) founding the Non-Aligned Movement in 1961

496. During the late 1960s, the Spanish government passed all these major reforms EXCEPT

(A) relaxing government controls on the press

(B) opening up a minority of seats in the Cortés to free election

(C) reducing the prominence of the Falange Party

(D) legitimizing non-Catholic organizations that had had to operate underground

(E) granting of many civil and individual rights and freedoms

497. What was the result of the Velvet Revolution in Czechoslovakia?

(A) Czechoslovakia split into two independent republics.

(B) Vaclav Havel became president of Czechoslovakia in a free election.

(C) Soviet troops forced a regime change on Czechoslovakia.

(D) The Czechoslovakian leaders accepted aid from the Marshall Plan.

(E) Czechoslovakia joined the European Union.

498. The government imposed martial law throughout Poland in December 1981 in order to avoid all of the following EXCEPT

(A) invasion by the Soviet Union

(B) civil war

(C) planned free elections

(D) economic collapse

(E) a planned demonstration by Solidarity

499. Which was the last Eastern European nation to abandon Communism?

(A) Czechoslovakia

(B) East Germany

(C) Hungary

(D) Poland

(E) the Soviet Union

500. Mikhail Gorbachev's administration of the Soviet Union was different from the administrations of his predecessors in all these respects EXCEPT

(A) large amounts of money were invested in space exploration
(B) censorship was substantially relaxed
(C) one-party rule was ended
(D) the legislature was given real governing power
(E) the Soviet Union ceased to administer outside nations

ANSWERS

Chapter 1: Europe Enters the Modern Era

1. (A) The plagues originated in the Crimea. They were brought west on trading ships by infected rats and mice.

2. (D) The Church was by far the most powerful authority in Western Europe, but it was utterly helpless to do anything to combat the Black Death. This clearly showed that its claims of omnipotence were false.

3. (C) The original Christian Church had split into two denominations, corresponding to the two divisions of the Roman Empire: Eastern Orthodox, headquartered in Constantinople, and Roman Catholic, headquartered in Rome. The Council of Florence was convened in the hope of reuniting the denominations under one pope. The attempt failed; the denominations remain separate to this day.

4. (A) Machiavelli shocked the reading public with his bold assertion that a ruler should ignore ethical and moral considerations if they interfered with the maintenance of his power and authority. Until Machiavelli, people had at least paid lip service to the notion that a ruler must follow Christian principles of morality and honest dealing.

5. (C) Michelangelo is considered the greatest sculptor of his era. The frescoes he painted on the Sistine Chapel ceiling are among the towering achievements of art. His sonnets remain in print today in many languages. He is among the architects who reconstructed and restored the Vatican during the 16th century.

6. (E) The importance of being able to read and thus think for oneself cannot be underestimated. The printing press made literacy possible; with literacy, the great ideas and thoughts of humankind were available to everyone. Anyone who could read could now think for himself or herself about these ideas, instead of simply accepting whatever the authority figures decreed was true.

7. (C) Roman texts were written in Latin, which every educated Renaissance European could read. Greek texts were written in Greek, which most could not read. In addition, the Roman Empire had been centered in Italy, so the Roman texts were physically within easy reach of Western Europeans. Only travel and time would bring Greek texts to the West.

8. (D) Many European cities outside Italy had famous universities by the time the Renaissance began: Salamanca, Paris, Edinburgh, Oxford, and Barcelona, to name only a few.

9. (E) The Church's evident helplessness in the face of the Black Death caused many to question its authority. Great families such as the Medici of Florence behaved like the equals of the Church fathers, even acquiring influence over them by lending the Church money. Ideas and ways of thinking from the classical past directly called many of the Church's teachings into question. The rise in literacy enabled ordinary people to interpret texts for themselves for the first time, instead of just accepting what they were told. All these factors combined to weaken the Church in the popular regard.

10. (E) The study of theology was the exclusive pursuit of men preparing to enter the Church. The seven liberal arts, once the approved course of study for free men of ancient Rome, constituted an alternative to theological studies.

11. (D) The merchant princes of Italy were practical men. Training in the seven liberal arts, which included mathematics, logic, and rhetoric, would be an excellent foundation for a young man going into politics, statesmanship, banking, trade, the law, or the military. The ability to speak well in public, to work with numbers, and to argue cogently would obviously be very helpful to any citizen who had a prominent role to play in public life.

12. (A) Brunelleschi is best known for the brick dome of the Florence Cathedral, still today considered one of the great marvels of engineering. Leonardo is widely considered one of the greatest artistic and scientific geniuses of Western history, both for the beauty of his paintings and the breadth of his scientific knowledge and imagination. Dante is most famous for *The Divine Comedy*, a classic allegorical epic. Petrarch invented the sonnet form that poets throughout the Western world continue to use in their lyric poetry. Henri Matisse is from a different country and a much later era: he was a French painter of the Post-Impressionist school of the early 20th century.

13. (A) Italy had once been the heart of the Roman Empire and would become a unified nation-state in 1860. At the time of the Renaissance, though, the word *Italy* was a geographical term, not a political one. Politically, the Italian people were divided among a number of city-states and small kingdoms that were ruled independently. The Italians were linked by a common cultural and historical heritage, a common language (albeit with many regional dialects), and a common religious faith, but they were not politically unified.

14. (E) The merchant princes of Italy, such as the Sforzas and the Medici, used their wealth to gain enormous political power. Any vastly wealthy citizen in any nation is always respected and even feared by authority figures and people of high social standing. Because of their wealth, the merchant princes gained political power and power over the Church. They also used their money to sponsor major artistic and architectural projects and to sponsor gatherings such as the Council of Florence.

15. (A) Calvin had to flee his native France because Protestantism was not tolerated there. His ideas were received much more warmly in Geneva.

16. (B) The Ninety-Five Theses were propositions for debate. Luther was a devout Catholic who regarded the Church of his day as corrupt; he wanted to stir up a public debate that would bring about reform within the Church. He had no idea that he would end by creating a new denomination.

17. (A) The French monarchy did not tolerate Protestantism until near the end of the 16th century. The St. Bartholomew's Day Massacre is the most notorious and spectacular incident of the persecution of Protestants in France.

18. (C) The diet was an official gathering of the princes of the Holy Roman Empire in the town of Worms. The emperor ordered Luther to recant his statements about the Church. When Luther refused to recant, he was banished from the empire, but the elector of Saxony intervened and offered Luther protection in his own house.

19. (C) Originally, a *Protestant* was one who *protested* the Holy Roman Emperor's ban on Lutheranism.

20. (E) The principle of state sovereignty established in the Peace of Augsburg was captured in a Latin phrase of the time. *Cuius regio, eius religio* means "Whose realm, his religion"—in other words, each individual ruler could determine the faith of his own state.

21. (B) Calvinists (called Huguenots in France and Presbyterians in Scotland) believe that God predetermines each soul's fate before birth: that faith, good works, and sincere repentance cannot save anyone who is predestined to be damned.

22. (E) Predestination means just what the word says—that each individual's destiny is predetermined.

23. (B) The Edict of Nantes permitted all French citizens to worship as they saw fit, without fear of persecution.

24. (D) The Church, or at any rate its emissaries, had fallen into the practice of promising that indulgences could buy a donor heavenly forgiveness for sins. This outraged devout Catholics such as Luther, because the Church only had the power to waive earthly penance for sins. Only God had the power to waive punishment after the sinner died.

25. (C) To this day, Southern and Western Europe are predominantly Catholic; the Balkans and Eastern Europe are predominantly a mix of Catholic and Eastern Orthodox; and Germany, England, and Scandinavia are predominantly Protestant.

26. (E) Henry IV believed that forcing people to profess a faith they did not genuinely believe in would only lead to discontentment and rebellion. He felt that if people were allowed to have their own way in the matter of worship, they would be more contented and less likely to stir up political strife.

27. (C) The Reformation describes the creation of new Protestant denominations; thus the Counter-Reformation describes a variety of Catholic attempts to combat it.

28. (E) The Catholic Church had no authority to ban Protestantism anywhere; such a decision could only be made by a monarch.

29. (B) Calvinists and other extreme conservative Protestants, not Catholic orders, are the ones historically notable for preaching against dancing, singing, carousing, and gambling.

30. (A) The original purpose of the Roman Inquisition was to try Catholics accused of heresy. Choices B, D, and E more accurately describe the Spanish Inquisition, which reported directly to the Spanish monarch.

Chapter 2: Absolute Monarchy in Early Modern Europe

31. (C) Russia's bitterly cold winters proved a formidable barrier to frequent travel, and travel is a necessary condition for brisk mercantile trade.

32. (C) Russia had no balance of power in its government, only an autocrat. With no other branches of the government, there was no chain of command and no way to replace an unfit ruler.

33. (C) The Tatars had ruled Russia for many years. Only their departure allowed the Russians to begin ruling their own realm.

34. (A) Ivan IV distrusted the boyars, believing with justification that they would conspire against him if they had the chance; therefore he did not allow them any real authority or say in government.

35. (E) Wholesale executions and imprisonments took place briefly during the era of the *Oprichnina*, before the Time of Troubles, and would take place again under later Romanov czars, but these things were not a feature of the Time of Troubles itself.

36. (E) Muscovy's lack of natural barriers was both an advantage and a disadvantage; on the one hand, its central location allowed it to attack or expand in any direction, but on the other hand, it could be attacked or invaded from any direction. The best policy to pursue in this situation was to attack rather than wait to be attacked.

37. (B) First and foremost, the Russians had to drive out the Tatars in order to establish their own authority. Once the Tatars were gone, the next step was to unify the Russian principalities by establishing one ruling family in one capital city to rule over all. The ruling prince, later called *czar*, would cement his authority over all ranks of society, from the boyars to the peasants, and could then turn his attention to enlarging the empire with the purpose of becoming a major world power. Cultural exchange was much less important than any of these goals, although some degree of it did take place under Ivan III.

38. (D) Poland was eager to take advantage of Russia's period of unrest to strengthen its own position. When a usurper hoped to pass himself off as Czar Feodor's brother Dmitri, he offered the king of Poland certain territory in exchange for military support for his claim.

39. **(E)** The *Oprichnina* was a secret state police force created by Ivan IV. Like all such bodies in history—the Gestapo, for example—its members were universally hated and feared. Choices A and D are wrong because they presented no cause for resentment on anyone's part. Choice B is a false statement; Boris was a skilled administrator and a capable ruler. Choice C was nothing new in Russian politics; Ivan IV had distrusted the boyars and given them as little authority as he could.

40. **(B)** Boris restricted the peasants' right to move about freely in an attempt to quell the massive social unrest that was shaking the foundations of Russia at the time. First, the discontented aristocrats were pacified by obtaining greater control over the workers on their estates. Second, by restricting the peasants' mobility, the czar greatly reduced the likelihood of popular insurrection.

41. **(A)** Vasili II and his successors expanded the army by offering a powerful incentive to join—large tracts of land granted to the officer for his lifetime, and often to his heirs in perpetuity. The common people of Russia, by contrast, were required to serve in numbers proportional to the population of their locality.

42. **(E)** Ivan III invited a number of Western artists and architects to Russia; they entirely rebuilt the Kremlin, the fortified complex of buildings at the heart of Moscow. With its strikingly beautiful cathedrals, it has been a glorious symbol of Russia's power ever since.

43. **(E)** Most historians believe that Ivan suffered from severe mental illness and paranoia; his increasingly eccentric behavior and his suspicion of conspiracy on all sides are typical indicators. There is also some historical evidence that the czar was in constant pain from a debilitating spinal disease.

44. **(C)** In a system of absolute monarchy, the ruler's personality is the key to success. A capable ruler with vision and determination can make his or her state prosper: examples include Elizabeth I of England and Frederick II of Prussia. A weak, incompetent ruler ignores important matters that demand his or her attention, and the state generally slides into economic chaos and often into war. Examples include Ivan IV in his declining years, and Edward II of medieval England.

45. **(A)** The *Oprichnina* was a secret state police force. Ivan created it to spy on the people and to imprison, attack, or murder anyone who appeared to be guilty of disloyalty to Ivan personally or to the state (which of course Ivan regarded as one and the same). The *Oprichnina* reported directly to Ivan and was not subject to any law or authority other than the czar's whim. Its operatives can accurately be described as murderous thugs.

46. **(B)** The Spanish monarchs, having only recently united their kingdom, were determined to rule a religiously homogeneous people. They believed that a shared religious faith would create greater unity and minimize conflict among their subjects.

47. (D) Spain lost a vast number of ships and naval officers and men when the Armada was defeated. The defeat also constituted a loss of face for the monarch and the nation, because it was highly public; it was also the defeat of a large and powerful nation by a much smaller one.

48. (A) Henry VIII had divorced Mary's mother in order to marry Elizabeth's mother; Mary never forgave her mother's humiliation and never regarded her father's remarriage as valid (no Catholic with a living spouse could remarry unless the Church granted an annulment, which it denied to Henry). Elizabeth did not share her half-sister's religious beliefs; she was an observant although not a devout Anglican. All these factors made their relationship uneasy at best, hostile at worst.

49. (B) The same man ruled both kingdoms; he was King Charles I of Spain and Emperor Charles V of the Holy Roman Empire. Because Charles could not effectively govern both kingdoms simultaneously, he turned the Holy Roman Empire over to his brother, at first in fact and later in name as well. From the early 1500s onward, members of the same immediate family—the Hapsburgs—ruled both nations.

50. (A) Choices A through D all list major Spanish export products, but wool was by far the most important. Spanish sheep were a type that yielded Merino wool, which was highly sought after for its fine texture and quality. Choice E, wheat, is wrong because although some Spanish regions grew their own wheat, other regions had to import foreign wheat. The mountainous Spanish topography made it impossible to transport it any distance within the country.

51. (C) The idea behind the divine right of kings is that God chose to place the monarch in a position of supreme authority. To challenge the monarch, therefore, was to challenge the choice made by God—clearly untenable and blasphemous, because God was infallible.

52. (B) *Reconquista* means literally "reconquest." During the seventh century, the Muslims had expanded westward across North Africa and into the Iberian Peninsula; they held sway there for the better part of 800 years, until the Spaniards finally retook Granada, the last Muslim stronghold, in 1492.

53. (E) The Turks were determined to take the city of Vienna and expand northward into Europe. Repeated assaults on the city failed; Turkey did, however, gain quite a bit of territory in a peace treaty signed with Ferdinand I in 1547.

54. (C) Like all the Hapsburg family, Ferdinand was a Catholic who disapproved of Protestantism. However, unlike most of the family, he understood the political wisdom of religious tolerance. Ferdinand was open about his preference for ruling a Catholic realm, but he did not believe in wholesale religious conversion by force.

55. (A) The Holy Roman Empire was not a true empire. It was a loose association of independent kingdoms and city-states, each with its own independent monarch. In theory, these monarchs owed allegiance to the Holy Roman Emperor, whom they chose by election. In fact, the position of emperor was handed down from father to son like any other hereditary monarchy, and the kingdoms within the empire were frequently at odds with one another, particularly in the period beginning with the Reformation.

56. (E) Choice A is wrong because few if any hereditary monarchs had any experience of governing before they inherited the throne. Choice B is wrong because no such alternative existed; Spain had no parliament worthy of the name. Choice C is wrong because of the principle of rule by divine right; questioning Isabel's right to rule would have meant questioning God. Choice D is a false statement; many members of the Hapsburg family were afflicted with various mental illnesses, but Isabel was not. Isabel shared her authority with her husband because she considered it politically expedient; she was among the very first female monarchs in Europe, and she was not at all sure the people would accept her authority if it did not at least appear that she shared some of it with Ferdinand.

57. (B) Philip II was a devout Catholic, a meticulous and responsible administrator, and a humorless man. He resembled almost all his family in his refusal to tolerate Protestantism in his kingdom.

58. (A) The concept of an official language lay some distance in the future. Ferdinand ruled over a realm that embraced a number of languages and cultures—Czech, German, Hungarian, and Slav, among others.

59. (E) Spain had a thriving economy, especially once it acquired a colonial empire in the Americas. Great wealth came in from across the Atlantic, and at the same time Spain exported goods to other European nations.

60. (A) Isabel and Ferdinand arranged dynastic marriages for their children, who in turn did the same for their children. During this period, members of the Spanish royal family were connected by marriage to the thrones of England, Denmark, Hungary, France, and Portugal. The same family, the Hapsburgs, also ruled the Holy Roman Empire.

61. (C) Mary's persecution of Catholics earned her the nickname "Bloody Mary."

62. (A) King James I fit firmly into the tradition of absolute monarchs who believed in rule by divine right. James considered that in his person, he embodied the British state, and his will should not be shaped, questioned, crossed, or defied by any legislature. James believed that Parliament should be content to play its medieval role of rubber-stamping the monarch's requests for money to manage the kingdom's affairs.

63. (E) Henry VIII did not create the Anglican Church by royal command; Parliament created it according to the normal process of passing English legislation. The Act of Supremacy made the monarch Supreme Head of the Church in England. All four of the other choices happened before the Church of England was formally created.

64. (B) Elizabeth knew that she was an absolute monarch, but she also knew that absolute monarchs were sometimes overthrown or assassinated. In addition, she knew that her subjects might perceive her as weak simply because she was not a man. She courted the loyalty of the people in order to make herself more secure on her throne.

65. (E) Choice A is wrong because the English monarch was already much more powerful than Parliament. Choice B is wrong because since the loss of the Hundred Years' War with France, England's policies had generally reflected its geographical detachment from the rest of Europe. Choice C is a true statement, but was not the monarch's most important overall goal. Choice D is wrong because Elizabeth never fought a war of religion; this issue was unimportant to her.

66. (D) Benjamin Britten was England's greatest composer of the 20th century. The English Renaissance lasted from the reign of Henry VIII through that of James I; it is sometimes called the "Elizabethan Era" in literature and music because Elizabeth's reign marked its zenith.

67. (A) Henry VIII was a pragmatic ruler; he was also absolutely intolerant of opposition to his lightest wish. His wife Catherine had borne many children, but only one daughter had survived infancy. Henry wanted to divorce Catherine, marry Anne Boleyn, and father healthy sons to preserve the succession and avoid any possibility of civil war. Ironically, Anne Boleyn, like Catherine, bore only one daughter who lived to adulthood.

68. (A) England enlisted no allies to help it defeat Spain. The Spaniards had planned on support from the Netherlands once they actually invaded England, but they never got that far. The combination of strategy and better, lighter ships enabled the British to drive the Armada off. Having failed in a first attempt, the Armada was lost because possible reinforcements were too far away to come to the rescue, and because major sea storms destroyed many of the Spanish ships.

69. (B) The Thirty-Nine Articles set forth the doctrines of the Anglican Church, which all believers must agree to uphold. The articles were ratified as part of a religious settlement made when England abandoned the Catholicism it had resumed under Queen Mary and returned to Anglican worship. Under Edward VI, the document had included forty-two articles; some were abandoned, combined with others, or rewritten under Elizabeth because they were considered too Calvinist for England.

70. (D) Henry VII, who founded the Tudor dynasty, was the grandfather of Elizabeth and the great-grandfather of Mary Queen of Scots. Mary believed that her claim to the English throne was the stronger, because from the Catholic point of view Elizabeth was the illegitimate offspring of an invalid marriage (between Henry VIII and Anne Boleyn). The English people, however, did not support Mary; Elizabeth was a capable ruler, personally popular, and not Catholic. There were numerous plots against Elizabeth's life during her reign, and Mary was strongly believed to have participated in at least one of them.

71. (B) Choice A describes the King James Bible, Choice C the Vulgate Bible (a Latin translation in wide use at that time), Choice D *Foxe's Book of Martyrs*, and Choice E the Ninety-Five Theses. *The Book of Common Prayer* is the missal, or prayer book, to be used on a weekly basis in Anglican churches. It was highly significant because it was written in English, not Latin; it was a basic tenet of the Church of England that services must be conducted in the language of the people.

72. (C) When she became queen, Elizabeth was young, attractive, well-read, and lively. Her personal qualities and her royal status made her a very desirable marriage partner. Naturally, monarchs who proposed to Elizabeth (they included the kings of Spain and France) had to maintain a very friendly foreign policy toward England. Many historians believe that Elizabeth deliberately used her single status as a diplomatic tool; in addition, she likely had no inclination to share her royal authority with a husband. Choices A and E are wrong because the queen's marital status is irrelevant to them. Choice B is wrong because it affected domestic, not foreign, policy. Choice D assigns the wrong reason for any foreign assumptions about British weakness; foreign rulers tended to discount England because it was small and because it was an island.

73. (E) Both Catholics and low-church Anglicans felt the pressures of discrimination; the Catholics went so far as to plan to blow up the Houses of Parliament when the king and his ministers were in session. (The plot failed.) In northern Ireland, Protestants were expelling Catholic Irish from their land. The navy had received very little funding since its triumph over the Spanish Armada, and was in a highly dilapidated state. Parliament, which had enjoyed a certain amount of legislative power under Elizabeth, was restive under James's belief that it only existed to carry out the monarch's wishes.

74. (A) In medieval times, Parliament had only had one duty: to grant the monarch the funds necessary to keep the state functioning. For example, if the monarch planned to declare war, he or she had to request funding from Parliament. Over time, especially under Elizabeth I, Parliament had flexed its muscles; the members had come to believe they had the right to be consulted on—although not to dictate—national policy. James wanted to keep Parliament in its medieval role, believing as he did that he ruled by divine right and that Parliament had no right to question his will. James therefore dissolved Parliament in 1611 and did not summon it again for a decade; in 1621, desperately in need of finances, he summoned it again only to dissolve it again in anger.

75. (B) Once it conceded defeat in the Hundred Years' War and withdrew its claims to French territory, England avoided involvement in continental affairs until modern times. Sharing no borders with the great European monarchies, England had little reason to get involved in their conflicts with one another. The geographical fact that England was an island explains its political isolation.

76. (A) The Defenestration of Prague is the name for an incident that took place one day in Prague Castle, when a group of government-hating Lutherans literally shoved some of the Catholic civil servants through the windows on the upper floors. (*Fenestra* is Latin for "window.") Ferdinand Hapsburg, the newly crowned king of Bohemia, was a Catholic, and had begun his reign by revoking many rights and privileges that had been extended to Protestants in 1609. The Defenestration of Prague touched off a major Protestant uprising, leading to the ouster of Ferdinand and the declaration of war.

77. (B) Geography is a very important element in the history of all European nations. No nation would want to lie geographically between two strong nations that were allies of one another; the nation in the middle would clearly be highly vulnerable to invasion, takeover, and partition. France's goal in the Thirty Years' War was to strengthen its own position by making sure of two things: first, that its neighbors not become too strong, and second, that its neighbors not form alliances that would weaken France.

78. (E) Gustav II Adolph's death on the battlefield did not end Sweden's participation in the war. His brilliant military commanders carried on the fight, and his daughter Kristina ruled Sweden and managed the war with the advice of her chief minister, Axel Oxenstierna. By 1647, the Swedish troops had reached Prague; the following year, the Peace of Westphalia granted Sweden several desirable territories.

79. (C) All of the fighting had taken place in the north central European region that would later become Germany and Austria. Historians estimate that between one-fifth and one-third of the total ethnic German population was killed in the war; in addition, the land had been laid waste and bands of foreign mercenaries who survived the war were roaming the devastated land to loot, burn, and kill.

80. (D) Some groups within the Holy Roman Empire went to war in the name of religious freedom, but they were not attempting to change their rulers or systems of government.

81. (B) The political and religious situation in Bohemia resulted in a mostly Lutheran landed aristocracy chafing under the authority of a mostly Catholic bureaucracy. The tension between the two groups resulted in the Defenestration of Prague—the event historians consider the first conflict of the war.

82. (C) France was geographically vulnerable, caught between two large allied nations: Spain to the southwest and the Holy Roman Empire to the east. If the Holy Roman Empire became a strong, unified nation, this would weaken France; therefore France's main motivation was to fight against the emperor and his allies. This meant fighting on the Protestant side.

83. (E) Sweden's military successes in the war brought it much valuable territory and made it, briefly, a great power in Europe.

84. (A) The Peace of Westphalia did not change or establish any rules for eligibility for the post of Holy Roman Emperor, which at the time was generally handed down from one direct heir to the next in the Catholic Hapsburg family.

85. (C) The Holy Roman Empire was severely weakened by the war; France, by contrast, was a nation-state with a strong monarchy, able ministers, a large land mass, and a central location on the European map. It would dominate Europe until 1815.

86. (B) The end of the Thirty Years' War was the first time that all the combatants of a war fought among many nations met to discuss and agree on a peace that tried to achieve a balance of power among all of them.

87. (C) The Thirty Years' War showed that armies had grown much less mobile than they had been during the Hundred Years' War (fought between England and France in the 14th and 15th centuries). The introduction of heavy artillery, the arming of the infantry and cavalry, and the vast increase in the number of troops all resulted in making warfare more static and less mobile.

88. (B) The Letter of Majesty, issued in 1609, had granted a number of important rights and privileges to Protestants within Bohemia, despite the fact that Catholicism remained the state religion. When Ferdinand revoked the edict, he aroused not only the wrath but the active opposition of the Protestants whose rights he was taking away.

89. (C) Spain had long since begun the process of colonizing the Americas, but it had no reason to send massive numbers of troops across the Atlantic; its ventures into America went unchallenged by the other European powers for some time.

90. (A) At the end of the war, the Hapsburgs found themselves monarchs of the Empire of Austria, created from the southern and eastern parts of the Holy Roman Empire. Tens of thousands of Bohemian and Austrian Protestants emigrated from the new nation rather than converting to Catholicism; others were willing to observe Catholicism outwardly; still others converted voluntarily and wholeheartedly. The end result was that Austria was a largely Catholic empire.

91. (A) When Charles I became king, he asked Parliament to grant him the right to collect import duties throughout his reign, as had historically been the custom. Smarting over its disrespectful treatment at the hands of James I, Parliament agreed to grant James's son these tax-collecting rights for only one year. Charles dissolved Parliament and collected the taxes without its permission, throwing people who would not pay into prison. Charles was forced to reconvene Parliament in 1628; the members presented him with the Petition of Right, which reminded the king that according to the Magna Carta and laws passed under Edward III, Englishmen could not be taxed without their own consent—that is, the consent of their elected representatives in Parliament.

92. (C) A high-church Anglican is one who prefers pomp and ceremony in the worship service; a low-church Anglican prefers a much more spartan style of worship. Thus, low Anglicans of the period shunned high Anglicans as being almost as corrupt as Catholics, while high Anglicans scoffed at low Anglicans for being as joyless and stern as Presbyterians. The name "Puritan" comes from the low-church Anglican desire to *purify* the Church of England from corrupting Catholic influence.

93. (B) During Elizabeth's long reign, Parliament had grown accustomed to being consulted on national policy. The legislators did not question the monarch's right to make all the final decisions, but they expected to be consulted. They had not reacted well to James's failure to treat them with respect and allow them their due measure of participation in the government; when Charles I proved equally uncompromising, they went to war against him and eventually ordered his execution. With another regime change in 1689 and the passage of the English Bill of Rights, Parliament became the supreme law of the land. From that time forward, England was a constitutional monarchy in which the monarch had less and less say in national policy.

94. (A) Charles I and Archbishop of Canterbury William Laud believed that it was their duty to unify Scotland and England religiously. (Charles was, of course, hereditary monarch of both Scotland and England, as his father, James I, had been before him.) Because Laud and the king both preferred the high-church Anglican rites, these were the ones they imposed on the Church of Scotland. This was unpalatable to the Scots for two reasons. First, the Church of Scotland was not Anglican at all, but Presbyterian; second, Presbyterianism was spiritually akin to low-church Anglicanism. Therefore, this ill-advised attempt to overthrow the national church resulted in armed invasion.

95. (D) Cromwell's official title was "Lord Protector of the Commonwealth" (in the wake of Charles I's execution, Parliament abolished the monarchy). His swift and brutal way of dealing with his opponents marked him from the start as a military dictator. After a series of increasing conflicts with Parliament over reforms that he supported and the legislators opposed, he instituted direct military rule.

96. (A) The Bill of Rights was a direct result of the Glorious Revolution, which brought about a peaceful dynastic change in England and introduced the era of constitutional monarchy.

97. (B) Charles I was a quiet, shy, studious man; like many such, he found it very difficult to be genial, friendly, or relaxed in his face-to-face dealings with people. Politically, he would not or could not move with the tide of history; he believed he ruled by divine right, and that to give up any part of his authority to Parliament was to defy God's will. His wife Henrietta Maria gave birth to several healthy children; the king's subjects looked askance on the possibility of being ruled one day by a monarch who had been raised as a Catholic. Finally, Charles's high-church Anglican beliefs clashed with the increasing popularity of low-church Anglicanism, also called Puritanism.

98. (C) Ironically, since the basic reason for deposing Charles I had been his refusal to cooperate with Parliament, Cromwell found himself as much at odds with the House of Commons as the king had been. Exasperated at Parliament's refusal to pass his program of reforms, Cromwell disbanded it and ruled more or less by military decree until his death in 1658.

99. (E) Anti-Catholic feeling ran very high in England during the 17th century; the English had looked with disfavor on Charles I's queen, Henrietta Maria, because she was a Catholic and would probably raise her children in that faith. Her eldest son Charles II was content to observe the Anglican religion, but his brother and heir James was a Catholic. The Exclusion Bill was an attempt to *exclude* James from the succession on those grounds. Charles II dissolved Parliament twice in response to the bill; it eventually passed the House of Commons but failed to pass the House of Lords, and James II was crowned in 1685.

100. (D) Charles I was forced to summon Parliament in November 1640; this "Long Parliament," named for the eight-year length of its session, immediately agitated for a number of changes in the government that would expand its powers and reduce the monarch's. Charles agreed to several of the new laws, such as the Triennial Act described in Choice A, but balked at others, including a bill that robbed the monarch of his authority to command the armed forces. When negotiations between king and Parliament reached an impasse, Parliament defied the king, declaring publicly that the monarch's consent to its acts was unnecessary. Charles I's response was to raise an army and march against Parliament, thus beginning the Civil War.

101. (B) The Glorious Revolution was not a war, but a change in monarchs that came about without a shot being fired. James II fled England when Parliament brought in his daughter Mary and her husband William, *stadholder* (hereditary ruler) of the Netherlands, as England's new constitutional monarchs.

102. (A) A severe outbreak of the plague occurred during the 1660s; the historic Great Fire of London was fortunately timed because it destroyed thousands of the rats and other vermin that carried the disease. Planning for St. Paul's Cathedral, notable for its neoclassical style and its vast dome, was begun in 1666; the foundation stone was laid, possibly by the king himself, in 1675. Where most of the great cathedrals of the world took at least a century to complete, architect Sir Christopher Wren oversaw the completion of his masterpiece during his own lifetime. Wren was a member of the Royal Society, to which Charles II granted an official charter; fellow members included John Locke, Isaac Newton, and other notable figures in philosophy, letters, science, and the arts.

103. (B) The Declaration of Indulgence specifically stated that since the previous four reigns had proved that religious worship could not be forced or legislated, all citizens should be free to worship either at home or in public, professing any faith they chose, as long as their religion did not attempt to undermine the government. The document echoed the tolerance of the Roman Empire and was an important precursor to the First Amendment to the U.S. Constitution, with its guarantee that the nation would never establish an official religion. Presbyterians in Scotland and Anglicans in England regarded the Declaration of Indulgence with hostility, suspicious that its true purpose was to undermine their own powerful churches. In the end, the document ceased to apply after James was deposed in 1689.

104. (E) The Cavaliers were the royalist side; the Roundheads, named for their short cropped haircuts, supported Parliament. Many people truly believed that raising one's sword against the monarch, however much they might disagree with him, was blasphemy or treason. Many people feared that the triumph of Puritanism would bring about an uprising of the lower classes. Many people believed, like Charles I, that the high-church Anglican style of worship represented the ideal middle ground between Catholicism and Calvinism, and they fought to defend it. Parliament announced it would seize the property of men who fought for the king; these men naturally took up arms against the Roundheads to defend their property. Choice E is the correct answer because Parliament made no such declaration.

105. (B) Charles II's reign is called the Restoration because his coronation *restored* the hereditary monarchy after England's only period of being ruled by a commoner (Oliver Cromwell). *Interregnum* is Latin for "between reigns" and refers to Cromwell's administration. The Glorious Revolution refers to the coronation of William and Mary. The term *Carolingian* does derive from the name Charles (*Carolus* in Latin), but historians use this term to refer to a French dynasty from the early medieval period. The Regency is a period in the early 19th century, when George III succumbed to mental illness and his son George IV ruled as the Prince Regent.

106. (B) Louis and his chief minister Jules Mazarin did not believe in sharing their power with the aristocracy or the people. Louis never convened the Estates General.

107. (E) Louis believed that if he kept the aristocrats under his personal eye at Versailles, they would not have the opportunity to hatch any kind of coup or conspiracy against him. Even if some of them had attempted to hold secret meetings at Versailles, the palace was full of loyal servants and spies who would have promptly reported any such meetings to the king.

108. (A) The Fronde was primarily a protest against new taxes levied on the common people to pay for a series of largely unsuccessful foreign wars.

109. (C) The close family tie between Louis XIV and the heir to the Spanish throne alarmed the other European powers, who foresaw a possible close alliance or even a formal union between Spain and France. Because these two nations were the greatest powers in Europe, the smaller nations united to prevent them from becoming a joint superpower.

110. (E) The French royal sponsorship of the arts and letters was highly unusual in Europe during the era; censorship was the usual rule. The French state's approving regard of its great men of letters greatly added to their social prestige and made them the celebrities of their day. This is one of a number of reasons that made Paris the hub of the Enlightenment.

111. (A) La Rochelle was a Huguenot stronghold on the Atlantic coast of France. Like the southern town of Montauban, it had its own local assembly and its own military. When France declared war on England in 1627, the mayor of La Rochelle allied himself with the British. The French army retaliated by laying siege to La Rochelle. The Peace of Alès ended the siege on terms that both sides could agree on; the Huguenots retained the freedom to worship as they pleased, but La Rochelle and Montauban lost their rights to self-government. The Huguenots repaid the terms of the treaty by becoming very loyal to the king.

112. (B) The moderation shown in the Peace of Alès did not remain royal policy for long. As the 17th century continued, the Huguenots saw more and more of their rights taken away. Some individuals were undoubtedly forced out of France on a religious basis, but this is the only one of the five choices that was not wholesale royal policy that affected all Huguenots.

113. (E) Richelieu and Mazarin were modern statesmen in many respects, but they firmly opposed giving any authority to a French legislature. As chief minister, Richelieu could govern France in close consultation with the king without opposition; his successor Mazarin also preferred to govern with no input except from the king. (The *intendants* were court-appointed agents whose job it was to travel into the provinces to ensure that local government offices were being run according to the rules.)

114. (E) The reverse of this statement is true. Under the king's chief minister, Jean-Baptiste Colbert, the French navy grew from fewer than 20 ships in 1661 to more than 275 ships in 1683. One of the reasons France was in serious financial trouble in the years leading to the Revolution is the amount of money spent on maintaining the navy. The army was substantially built up as well during this period, but not at the cost of expanding the navy.

115. (B) Choice B is the only one of the five that *cost* the government money rather than *saving* it money. Of course, it cost money to acquire colonies, to build the Canal du Midi, and to support specific luxury industries, but these were investments that brought immediate and substantial financial returns. Building the fortifications was simply one more foreign-policy choice, like the constant wars on which Louis XIV insisted, that drained the treasury.

116. (B) La Fontaine (1621–1695) is famous for his short stories and fables; he was the Aesop of his day. Jean Racine (1639–1699) and Molière (real name Jean-Baptiste Poquelin; 1622–1673) are two of the greatest playwrights in French history; Racine is known for his neoclassical tragedies, Molière for his satires. Marie de Rabutin-Chantal, the Marquise de Sévigné (1626–1696), is the author of a famous collection of letters that provide a lively record of France in the 17th century. Victor Hugo (1802–1885) was considered the greatest French author of the 19th century.

117. (C) The Dutch merchant fleet was among the largest and most successful in Europe at this period; the small size of the Netherlands enabled it to concentrate on economics rather than conquest, and thus it was wealthy and prosperous while most of the great military powers, such as France, were heavily in debt. France went to war in the hope of annexing the Netherlands and thus gaining a huge economic prize. Grabbing territory was not the goal; the goal was to add the Dutch wealth to the French treasury.

118. (A) Colbert was minister of finance; he can be fairly described as Louis XIV's chief accountant. Colbert's policies drastically reduced royal expenditures and also boosted income. For example, he oversaw the elimination of many royal annuities (thus saving the crown millions of *livres* a year) and established state support for industries such as textiles, thereby making them much more profitable and thus increasing revenue for the crown.

119. (B) Louis XIV was a great patron of the arts. The academies provided official status in many disciplines, along with a gathering place for the intellectuals and increased opportunities for learning and experiment. Financial support was of course welcome. Building projects such as Versailles and the completion and restoration of the Louvre were not mere construction projects to employ builders; they were serious attempts to create monumental works of art. The climate of royal support for the arts expressed in all these practical ways enticed many Italians and Germans to emigrate to France. Censorship, of course, ran counter to all of these positive policies.

120. (E) Choices A through D are all historically significant because they help explain why the French Revolution and the Terror took place. The required attendance at Versailles forced the aristocrats to waste their money on fine clothing and other nonessentials instead of investing it back into their estates. It also eroded the social contract of the time, in which the people served the landlord and the landlord protected and cared for the people. When the landlord regularly abandoned the estate for half the year, and stopped putting money into it, great resentment grew up among the peasants. Additionally, the custom of the time dictated that tradesmen would not demand payment from aristocrats, but would permit them to buy on credit, often for months or even years at a time. As unpaid bills to the skilled bourgeois upholsterers, wigmakers, tailors, and so forth mounted, so did middle-class resentment of the upper class.

121. (C) Joseph II's reign predates the concepts of economic nationalization and industrialization.

122. (E) Richard Strauss was born long after the classical era ended; he spans both the late Romantic and the Modern eras in music and was still active during World War II. The other four names are all roughly chronological contemporaries, and all spent many years of their highly successful musical careers in Vienna, which was the musical capital of Europe at that time.

123. (B) Holy Roman Emperor Charles V had no sons; therefore he had to take legal steps to ensure that his daughter Maria Theresa would be eligible to succeed to the throne of Austria after his death.

124. (D) Frederick was a highly able and effective ruler, and greatly enhanced Prussia's prestige. On his death, Prussia had achieved a status equal to that of Austria; however, France was still the dominant European power.

125. (B) Peter the Great was determined that Russia should take its place among the modern nations of Western Europe. The establishment of a new, architecturally beautiful and modern capital city in the westernmost part of the empire was only one of many steps Peter took to westernize Russia.

126. (E) It was during the 18th century that Prussia developed into a militaristic culture; this was a practical response to its vulnerable central location on the European continent. Other nations would always hesitate to attack any nation with an impressive army.

127. (E) As conservatives have done in all cultures throughout history, the conservatives of Joseph's Austria strongly opposed reform. Conservatives oppose reform because it tends to equalize economic and social classes; they do not welcome this enforced sharing of what they regard as their exclusive rights and privileges.

128. (A) The Eastern Orthodox Church underwent a schism in 1667 when it excommunicated the leaders of the conservative, anti-reform faction who would become known as the Old Believers. The Old Believers were opposed to any westernization of the Orthodox Church as it existed in Russia—even to reforms that would have brought the Russian liturgy, scriptures, and rites more into conformity with Eastern Orthodoxy as it had developed in Greece and in the now-defunct Byzantine Empire. Catherine the Great accomplished much during her reign, but she did not succeed in mending the Orthodox schism.

129. (E) The old principalities of Brandenburg and East Prussia had been divided by a wide, irregularly shaped swath of land bisected by the Vistula River. This was the land Prussia took during the First Partition of Poland, and renamed West Prussia. Frederick's goal was to strengthen his kingdom by unifying it geographically.

130. (E) Prussia was a conservative monarchy that believed in the system of absolute hereditary rule. A strong legislature and a written constitution did not belong to this picture.

131. (B) Peter did take the field during the climactic Battle of Poltava, but the czar was not the commander-in-chief of the Russian forces; he had a staff of able generals headed by the experienced Boris Sheremetev. All the other factors combined to spell defeat for Sweden.

132. (B) Prussia would never have become a strong kingdom on its own, or the core of the powerful nation of Germany, without the strong and decisive leadership of its highly able kings and later its chief ministers. Geography was a major factor in Prussian policy. Prussia was a small, centrally located state with no natural borders to defend it. Its choice was either to capitulate to invading powers, as Poland would do in the late 1700s, or to make other nations hesitate to invade it by building up its own army. The Hohenzollern kings made the latter choice; by the mid-1700s Prussia had one of the most impressive and respected armies in Europe.

133. (C) Prussia did come to Austria's aid in the war, which lasted until 1699 and resulted in Austria's acquisition of a great deal of Hungarian territory, but the two great powers did not form a lasting alliance. At times they were allies and at times they were enemies.

134. (D) The early Romanov czars and empresses had chief ministers, some of whom wielded considerable influence, and they sometimes established councils to address specific issues in committee. However, this was as far as the Russian monarchs went toward sharing their power. Russia never had a strong legislature at any time in its history.

135. (A) Joseph II can be compared to the father of an 18th-century European family—convinced that it was his responsibility to provide for and take care of his wife and children, and their responsibility to give him their obedience and loyalty. Joseph ruled as an autocrat not because he had the inclinations of a tyrant, but because he believed that the monarch, like the head of a household, *must* know better than the people what was best for them—and that it was his duty to take care of his people.

136. (D) Prussia, Austria, and all the smaller states of the Holy Roman Empire all experienced a surge in education at this time—but not among the lower classes. The educated elite class grew, and became much more vocal and influential; the peasants, however, remained untouched by this development. In the late 1700s, "Germany" was still a cultural and linguistic entity rather than a political or national one.

137. (C) Poland had been a strong monarchy during the Middle Ages, but gradually fell more and more under the sway of the surrounding powers. Swedish troops occupied Poland during the 1650s, and much of the Great Northern War was fought on Polish territory. Russia made Poland a protectorate in 1717, but this status did not last; in the 1760s, Catherine the Great used her intimate personal relationship with Poland's King Stanislav to take over half of Poland. In 1772, 1793, and 1795, Austria, Prussia, and Russia divided Poland among themselves in what historians refer to as the First, Second, and Third Partitions of Poland. Russia took over by far the largest share of the three. The nation of Poland would not reappear on the European map until after World War I.

138. (E) The Streltsy was founded in the early 1600s as a special semi-regular military unit whose job was to defend the court and the borders. These troops were a special source of resentment for the people, because special "Streltsy taxes" paid their salaries and expenses. Under Feodor, these taxes were eliminated, but the Streltsy regiment itself was not disbanded.

139. (C) Prussia had gained the rich province of Silesia in a surprise attack on Austria in 1740–1742; Frederick the Great had to engage in a Second Silesian War in 1744–1745 to keep the territory. Austria marched against Prussia again in 1756, determined to regain Silesia. France and Russia allied with Austria, believing that Prussia was growing much too strong. The war ended in a victory for Prussia.

140. (B) Sweden, Russia, and France all had strong vested interests in crushing Prussia; Prussia threatened all three nations because it was in a good geographical location to attack any one of them, and it possessed one of Europe's strongest and most formidable armies.

141. (C) Peter believed that westernization would be good for Russia in trade, in economics, militarily, politically, and culturally. It would not, however, help Russia expand its eastern borders.

142. (D) Maria Theresa was an admirably enlightened ruler in most respects, but she did harbor religious prejudices against all non-Catholics. One example of this is the banishment of Jews from Prague that took place by her order between 1744 and 1748.

143. (A) Prussia became a major European power almost overnight with the seizure of Silesia. This meant that there were now two strong German powers in central Europe—Austria and Prussia—where there had been only one. Austria viewed Prussia as a serious threat.

144. (A) Razin was a Cossack from the Ukrainian region. In the wake of a war against Poland, a period of unrest arose in the Don Cossack region south of Moscow, and Razin led a large band of the Cossacks through the countryside on a mission of plunder. Around 1670, the looting and theft turned into a political uprising against the repressive policies of the landowning class and the state. Although Razin attracted thousands of Cossack and Russian followers, he had no clearly defined political goals. He was betrayed, captured, and executed in 1671.

145. (E) The Silesian Wars were territorial wars between Austria and Prussia. The resulting peace treaty gave most of the province of Silesia to Prussia in exchange for Prussian recognition of Maria Theresa as the legitimate empress of Austria, and of her husband Francis Stephen of Lorraine as Holy Roman Emperor.

146. (A) The dual monarchy of Austria-Hungary would not be created until the mid-19th century. According to the agreement of 1687, the kingdom of Hungary was a part of the Austrian Empire, although the emperor agreed to uphold its constitution and grant its Protestant citizens the right to worship as they saw fit.

147. (C) By invading Prussia and the small independent German states, Napoleon unwittingly helped to give rise to German nationalism. The reorganization of the bureaucracies, the writing of new constitutions, and the modernization of the law codes benefited the German states in the long run, but no nation has ever enjoyed having such things imposed on it by foreign conquerors. When Russia defeated Napoleon and the Grand Army, Prussians reacted with joy, and swiftly took up arms to fight for their own independence from France. The Prussian army would play a major role in Napoleon's final defeat at Waterloo in 1815.

148. (A) Peter was characterized by genuine scientific and intellectual curiosity, and equally by his determination to see that Russia took its political and cultural place among the great European powers. With this in mind, he traveled through Western Europe with a large entourage. The goals of the mission were to achieve meaningful diplomatic and political exchange, to expose Russian officials to Western methods and ideas, and to interest Europeans in traveling to Russia to play major roles in its modernization. There was no thought of uniting the two major Catholic denominations.

149. (E) Choices A through D describe the major problems that kept the Holy Roman Empire from becoming a powerful nation-state in the era before German unification. First, the war had devastated both the population and the land. Second, since each of the many small city-states and kingdoms within the empire was independent, trade was an inefficient and expensive process. Third, while other European nations were growing rich from their colonial empires, the Holy Roman Empire faced both geographical and military obstacles to sailing west and building an empire. Fourth, the individual components of the empire were simply too small to have large economies. Together, as a united Germany, they would prove to be economically strong; as the Holy Roman Empire they were divided and weak. Linguistic and cultural diversity did exist within the empire, but cultural diversity was only an explosive force in a centralized state with large, vocal minorities. The Holy Roman Empire was not a centralized state, hence the various cultural and ethnic groups were not placed into competition with one another.

150. (C) Leif Eriksson was a Norseman; he landed on the Canadian coast around the year AD 1000, but he and his people did not attempt repeat voyages or colonization. Cortés led the conquest of the Aztecs in Mexico and claimed their lands for Spain. Menendez de Avilés established the first permanent Spanish settlement in North America. Raleigh claimed the territory of Virginia in the name of Elizabeth I. Winthrop was the first governor of the Massachusetts Bay Colony and thus one of the men most responsible for creating a stable, viable British presence in North America.

151. (D) British and colonial troops defeated the French in Canada. As a result of the war, France gave up all of its claims to colonies on the North American continent.

152. (E) Isabel of Spain sponsored the voyages of Christopher Columbus, of which the first was in 1492.

153. (C) Lack of opportunity at home was the primary motivation for emigration from Europe to the United States in the 19th and 20th centuries, but it was not a major factor during this early era of exploration.

154. (A) The most important factor in the conquest of the Americas was the difference in weapons on the opposing sides. The people of the Americas had no modern weapons to compare with the European guns.

155. (C) Portugal was not a major European power that wanted to expand its sphere of political influence; it was a small nation that wanted to strengthen its economy by acquiring control of major trade routes between East and West.

156. (E) The location of present-day Pittsburgh on the Pennsylvania-Ohio border is the site of the first battle of the French and Indian War.

157. (A) Magellan himself did not survive the voyage, but several of his crew members did reach home safely after a three-year voyage. This voyage was the first to establish positively that it was possible to reach the East by sailing west.

158. (C) The Dutch did not pay cash for Asian goods; they offered their own goods for barter, just as the Portuguese did. The difference was that the Asians preferred Dutch goods to Portuguese ones.

159. (B) The native populations of the Americas had never been exposed to diseases such as smallpox; therefore they had no resistance to them. Tens of thousands of them died from smallpox and other diseases; therefore the Europeans had to find an alternative source of cheap labor.

160. (C) Pizarro led the conquest of the mighty Inca empire in the area that later became the nation of Peru, in the Cuzco Valley and the Andes Mountains.

161. (D) The French did build settlements in Canada, but their primary motivation in traveling to North America was mercantile. Frenchmen who went to North America did so in order to build up a highly profitable industry in the fur trade.

162. (B) Champlain was a Frenchman who crossed the Atlantic in 1603 and helped to found the French Canadian settlements of Port Royal and Quebec. He is also famous as the first European known to have seen the Great Lakes, as a cartographer who made early maps of the St. Lawrence River and the Atlantic coast, and as the leader whose friendly relations with the local Algonquin tribes led to a French and Indian alliance in the war against the British that would begin in 1754.

163. (A) Parliament argued that as the British legislative assembly, it represented all citizens of the British Empire—those who did not have actual voting members for their districts were "virtually represented" by the entire Parliament. The North American colonists argued that with no actual members of Parliament representing their specific interests, they were not bound to obey parliamentary laws. The colonists cited provisions in the Magna Carta—signed by King John in the year 1215—that established the tradition of taxation only by general consent of the citizens, and of the right to a trial by a jury of one's peers. When Parliament began passing laws taking away these rights, the colonists took up arms against Britain in what became known as the American Revolution.

164. (A) France ceded all territory east of the Mississippi River (except the port of New Orleans) to Britain, and all territory west of the Mississippi to Spain. France divided the territory in order to prevent Britain from taking over the entire continent at once. When France later seized control of Spain, Napoleon took back the territory west of the river; in 1803, he sold it outright to the United States in a transaction known as the Louisiana Purchase.

165. (A) Da Gama discovered that he could reach India by rounding the southern tip of Africa and then sailing northeast. Beginning in 1505, Portugal made full use of his discovery to set up trading posts throughout Southeast Asia.

Chapter 3: The Era of Political and Intellectual Revolution

166. (D) Copernicus first suggested the theory of a solar system, and Brahe and Kepler agreed with this theory, but Galileo was the first to look through a telescope and prove it.

167. (B) Galileo pointed out that what people could perceive with their five senses was obviously real and factual. He argued that if the evidence of the human eye appeared to conflict with Holy Scripture, then Holy Scripture was being misinterpreted.

168. (A) Technological advances such as the invention of the telescope made it possible for the modern scientists to observe things that were invisible to the ancients.

169. (B) The Church hierarchy had been the most powerful authority in Western Europe for a thousand years. Naturally, the clergy were very reluctant to cede any of that authority without a fight to keep it.

170. (C) The law of gravity explains that there is a scientific force that holds all the objects in the universe together, in specific relationships with one another. Gravity keeps the planets in orbit and the stars at fixed distances from one another. Gravity causes dropped objects to fall to Earth, and it prevents people from floating in the air. This one universal principle allowed human beings to understand that the universe, previously mysterious and unknowable, could be comprehended by all.

171. (E) Gravity is what governs the ebb and flow of the tide; this was part and parcel of the discoveries of Isaac Newton, who was born the year Galileo died.

172. (B) Isaac Newton's experiments with light and light prisms clarified the nature of reflection and refraction and explained in scientific terms what caused the phenomenon of the rainbow.

173. (A) Galileo discovered the moons of Jupiter by the simple means of looking repeatedly through his telescope and noticing that the stars near Jupiter changed position over time; what he saw told him that Jupiter had its own moons in orbit around it.

174. (A) In ancient times, Ptolemy had theorized that the sun and all the other heavenly bodies orbited the Earth; Copernicus was the first to suggest in print that Ptolemy was wrong and that the sun, not the Earth, was at the center. Copernicus arrived at this theory in an attempt to explain why the planets' orbits appeared irregular; he suggested that if the sun rather than the Earth were at the center, the orbits would appear regular.

175. (A) Bacon argued that the scientist must note actual, concrete observations and draw conclusions from them. In other words, the starting point for all scientific investigation was to gather data based on what scientists could perceive through their five senses, then to use that data to draw logical conclusions. Bacon was not the first scientist to espouse this method, but is considered its most vocal supporter.

176. (D) The Catholic Church taught that humankind was God's supreme creation, and thus was happy to accept the scientific theory that placed humankind at the center of all creation.

177. (E) Galileo was a devout Catholic throughout his long life, despite his treatment at the hands of the Roman Inquisition. Like most other figures of the Scientific Revolution, he believed in God and had great respect for the Bible and its teachings. Galileo knew that what the human eye could see through a telescope must be the truth, whereas any given passage in the Bible might be interpreted in many different ways. He argued that while fallible human beings could easily misinterpret the word of God, they could not deny the reality they perceived through their five senses. Thus science and religion were perfectly compatible; those who found them incompatible misunderstood the true meaning of the Scriptures.

178. (D) Descartes (1596–1650) was a pioneer in the field of analytical geometry, and also the most prominent proponent of the scientific method of starting from unarguable facts and researching from them toward logical conclusions. Among his other discoveries in astronomy and physics, Galileo (1564–1642) was the first to look through a telescope and thus disprove once and for all that the Earth was at the center of the universe. Halley (1656–1742) would today be called a geophysicist; he was also an astronomer who first calculated the orbit of the comet that bears his name. Picard (1620–1682) made many important contributions to astronomy, of which his best-known is measuring the circumference of the Earth to within a fraction of exact accuracy. Pepys (1633–1703) was not a scientist at all; he is famous for his gossipy, entertaining diary, which provides a lively, detailed, and colorful account of Europe, specifically London, during the 1660s.

179. (E) "Natural philosophy" was the 17th-century scientists' name for what we call physics. Other scientists besides Newton had worked on and begun to understand various aspects of physics, but *Principia Mathematica* was the first book to pull all of these diverse findings together and explain physics as an organic whole.

180. (B) Newton, Picard, Halley, Jean Richer, and others all noticed variations in the swing of a pendulum; the farther the pendulum was from the equator, the more slowly it would swing. Since gravity controlled the swing of a pendulum, this meant there was less gravity at the equator than at the poles, which in turn meant that the Earth was not a perfect sphere, but bulged slightly at the equator. *Oblate spheroid* is the scientific term for this shape. This theory was confirmed by separate experiments carried out in the 1730s.

181. (D) The French word *philosophe* does not mean the same thing as the English word "philosopher." It refers to an intellectual of the Enlightenment who applied a process of critical reasoning to social problems.

182. (C) Choice A is wrong because the *philosophes* were men (and some women) of many walks of life, from playwrights to statesmen. Choice B is wrong because the Enlightenment was an international phenomenon. Choice D is wrong because only the most idealistic of the *philosophes* preached against all war. Choice E is wrong because many of the *philosophes* were educated at the finest universities of the time.

183. (C) The purpose behind the *Encyclopédie* was to gather in one place all human knowledge about a variety of historical, scientific, artistic, and philosophical topics. With such a source of information, anyone who could read could become educated.

184. (A) The government of the United States of America, formed in the wake of the Enlightenment, based its three-branch governmental structure, in which each branch has certain checks on the powers of the other two, on *The Spirit of Laws*.

185. (D) After numerous disastrous adventures, Candide and his friends settle on their own farm, where they undertake the practical work necessary to keep it running at a profit. Candide sums up what he has learned by saying "one must cultivate one's garden"—in other words, abstract philosophy as represented by his friend Pangloss is all very well, but philosophy is best applied to solving practical human problems in a practical manner.

186. (B) Rousseau reasoned that human nature was inherently noble and good, but had been warped and made greedy and selfish by an unfair system of social privileges given out on the basis of birth. Take away the social system, Rousseau argued, and you eliminate the greed and selfishness. The other *philosophes* scoffed at his ideas; they saw no evidence that people were inherently noble. They believed that universal education was the best way to solve the problems of humankind.

187. (E) The physical scientists of the Scientific Revolution and the social scientists of the Enlightenment shared the same thought process—the drawing of conclusions from direct observation, and the application of critical reasoning to any problem that they wanted to solve. They all certainly studied the ancients, but in the ancient world the process had been to draw conclusions from abstract thought rather than from direct observation.

188. (C) Choice C is an accurate description of Britain rather than France; the latter was a conservative, absolute monarchy until the French Revolution of 1789. Even then, France would struggle for many decades to establish a workable strong assembly of elected representatives.

189. (B) Although some of the Enlightenment *philosophes* were women, there was (at least among men, who had all the power) no general drive for women's equality at this period in European history. Mary Wollstonecraft's *A Vindication of the Rights of Woman* was one of the first published arguments for equality, and it did not appear in print until 1792.

190. (C) The French *philosophes* struggled under an absolutist government, strict censorship of the press, and a national church that had a stranglehold on many aspects of the everyday lives of the people. As of 1689, Britain had a balanced constitutional monarchy with a freely elected legislature; it also boasted a relatively free press and relative freedom to worship as one pleased. The *philosophes* considered Britain an ideal society because it permitted its people to think for themselves and it praised its scholars rather than throwing them into prison. There were strict limits to freedoms in Britain, of course—only a minority of men had the right to vote, and there was social and professional discrimination against non-Protestants—but British society was much freer than French.

191. (E) France did not establish its first public-school system until the reign of Napoleon. The other four choices all show that throughout France, people were reading and discussing the ideas of the Enlightenment. Naturally, exposure to these ideas was much greater in the cities than the countryside, because books and pamphlets were more readily available and there were more gathering places.

192. (C) The *philosophes* were optimistic about the future of humankind. They believed that just as the 17th-century scientists had solved major questions about the workings of the planets, they themselves could solve the great difficulties that made life a tragic struggle for most human beings. The problems of society—poverty, hunger, inequality, slavery, and war—could be solved if the human reasoning process was properly applied.

193. (A) One example of Choice B is Montesquieu's *Persian Letters*, published anonymously in the Netherlands in 1721. Two examples of Choice C are Voltaire's *Candide* and Cervantes's *Don Quixote*. One example of Choice D is Voltaire, who settled at Lake Geneva near the Swiss border. One example of Choice E is Denis Diderot, the moving spirit behind the *Encyclopédie*, who was imprisoned after the publication of a controversial essay known in English as "A Letter on the Blind."

194. (B) The key to the Romantic movement in literature (and art and music) is individual expression. The writer's goal is to express his or her own highly personal point of view, not to conform to the rules of a particular form. Rousseau's autobiography prefigures the Romantic movement because it is his attempt to portray his inner emotional self.

195. (D) Antonio Gramsci (1891–1937) was a highly important political thinker, but of a later era. He was an Italian Marxist philosopher. D'Alembert was a mathematician who co-edited the *Encyclopédie* with Diderot, until he abandoned the project in 1758. Locke was a political thinker best known for his theory that the human mind at birth was a *tabula rasa* (blank slate) and that experience shaped the person's identity and character. Statesman, printer, and author Benjamin Franklin followed Voltaire's dictum "one must cultivate one's garden" by founding America's first anti-slavery society and establishing public libraries, besides contributing to the Declaration of Independence and the U.S. Constitution. Voltaire, of course, was the elder statesman of the Enlightenment—the author of numerous works of fiction and nonfiction and the most prominent symbol of his age.

196. (B) The entrenched French aristocracy supported the old regime because it provided them with rights and privileges they did not want to give up.

197. (A) The First Estate included all members of the Catholic clergy, regardless of their rank or income. The Second Estate included all members of the hereditary nobility. The Third Estate, by far the largest, included all those who did not belong to the first two groups—everyone from wealthy merchants and professionals to the poorest urban and farm workers.

198. (E) France had never had a legislative assembly with any governing powers. The Estates General had no power to set policy, or even participate in its making; moreover, it had not even met since the early 1600s.

199. (D) Napoleon was a brilliant administrator; many systems and institutions that he put in place continue to govern France more than 200 years later.

200. (B) The king was faced with such a severe financial crisis that he had little choice but to seek help from the deputies of the Estates General.

201. (D) The Tennis-Court Oath led to the creation of the National Assembly, which swiftly won a few crucial concessions from the monarch, including tax relief and freedom of the press.

202. (C) The people of Paris did not barricade themselves inside the Bastille. Impatience made them take the rebellion into their own hands. They literally tore the prison officials to pieces in the open streets, they seized and made use of the weapons stored in the prison, and they reveled in an act of defiance against one of the oldest and most brutal symbols of the old regime.

203. (B) The Declaration of the Rights of Man and of the Citizen is exactly what its name implies. It is a list of 17 major civil and legal rights and responsibilities of the citizens.

204. (A) Many deputies had argued in favor of a constitutional monarchy, but when the king tried to escape, they knew that if they allowed him to live, he would do his best to persuade powerful allies to put down the rebellion and restore the old regime.

205. (A) Choice B is wrong because Louis had been married for some time before the Revolution took place. Choice C is wrong because he did sign the Declaration, albeit under protest. Choice D is wrong because his removal from the throne did not necessarily mean that the new leaders intended to put him to death. Choice E is wrong because the king did have legitimate heirs.

206. (C) At this time in history, France had no organized political parties comparable to the Whigs and Tories in London, or the Federalists and Democratic-Republicans in the United States. The Jacobins belonged to a radical club, the Girondins to a more moderate club.

207. (B) This statement accurately describes the Directory, but does not identify a cause for its failure.

208. (A) All five statements describe actions Napoleon took during his reign, but only Choice A identifies the Code Napoleon.

209. (E) Britain sent troops to the Iberian Peninsula to aid the Spanish and Portuguese troops. This event is known as the Peninsular War.

210. (E) Throughout history, people who enjoy prosperity and comfort under any given system of government resist change. Wealthy bourgeois and aristocrats had, as they saw it, no incentive to argue for social or political reform that would only have meant sharing their own wealth and power.

211. (A) The Committee of Public Safety was among the earliest Socialist governments in history. It did control prices; it did nationalize businesses; it did order numerous executions of so-called "enemies of the state"; and it did encourage young men to join the military. It waged war with gusto, but did not support popular uprisings elsewhere in Europe.

212. (D) Despite the fact that the entire Revolution was based on the extension of civil and political rights to all, women were one group that actually lost rights and freedoms under Napoleon.

213. (B) The British navy defeated the French navy at the Battle of Trafalgar. Napoleon was never able to invade England, and it would never have occurred to him to make Britain into an ally, as the two nations were long-standing enemies.

214. (D) The Berlin and Milan decrees were part of what was called the "Continental System." Defeated in his planned invasion of Britain, Napoleon proceeded to punish Britain economically by trying to sever its commercial and trade relationships with all the European nations. The policy failed because various nations refused to participate, and because there was too high a demand for British goods.

215. (C) Napoleon followed the same pattern in every invasion throughout his stunningly successful military career. His strategy failed spectacularly during the 1812 invasion of Russia.

216. (B) The War of 1812 did not involve any Russian allies coming to the rescue. The Russian army retreated eastward, into the depths of the nation, and waited for winter. When the French were forced to retreat westward, the Russians pursued them and chased them back over the border. Numerical differences between the armies was never an issue.

217. (A) Before the Napoleonic invasion, Spain had been an absolute monarchy. The monarchy was restored after the Peninsular War.

218. (D) Napoleon's escape from Elba and march into France immediately halted the negotiations at Versailles, where the national leaders summoned their generals to organize his swift defeat and recapture.

219. (B) The balance of power among nations was the key principle at stake during the Napoleonic Wars. The idea behind it was to prevent any one nation from growing so strong that it threatened all the others. When the French Empire threatened to take over Europe, the leaders worked together to oppose the takeover.

220. (E) The leaders at Vienna were for the most part monarchists, or at most constitutional monarchists. They were not liberal, republican, or democratic. The era of leaders recognizing and accommodating the forces of nationalism was still a little way in the future.

221. (B) The concordat was an agreement. The Directory had abolished the Church in France; Napoleon restored it because he understood that it was of great emotional importance to the people of France, as it had been their national church since the days of Charlemagne. He considered the Church valuable to the state as a unifying cultural force.

222. (E) Napoleon's loss to the allied armies under the command of the British Duke of Wellington and the Prussian General Blücher at the Battle of Waterloo gave us the idiom "meeting one's Waterloo," which signifies "facing one's final defeat."

223. (B) The poorer priests of the First Estate had a great deal in common with the poorer laypeople of the Third Estate. These were the two groups most interested in reform, because they suffered the most from the policies of the old regime.

224. (C) Hunger was the women's first concern. Theft and a bonfire might have appealed to them, but their immediate goal was to feed their families.

225. (B) France went through a series of constitutional monarchs, some of whom rolled back reforms and tried unsuccessfully to rule as autocrats. However, after the fall of Napoleon, France always had at least some degree of representation and a balance of powers in the government.

226. (B) There was no lack of great scientific minds in continental European nations. It is common sense that continental Europeans were just as scientifically curious and inventive as British ones; the Renaissance and the Scientific Revolution are proof of this. Economic, financial, and political considerations, not scientific ones, held Europe back while Britain moved forward.

227. (C) Factories in the Mediterranean had to depend on waterwheels and water turbines, because there was very little coal to be dug out of the ground. Northern France, England, Poland, and Germany, by contrast, were rich in coal deposits.

228. (E) This was not a cause of the enclosure movement, but rather something that worked hand in hand with it to make large-scale farming profitable.

229. (B) Jethro Tull invented a mechanical seed drill that could sow a field much more evenly and quickly than the old method of sowing by hand.

230. (D) Once Germany became a unified nation in 1871, it concentrated on improving its industry. It had once produced only half the amount of coal mined in Britain; by 1914, it was producing twice as much.

231. (C) The development of the railway made the distribution of goods easier and more efficient, but did not affect the manufacturing process. The inventions listed in Choices A, B, D, and E all made the spinning and weaving process much more efficient and greatly increased the output of the textile mills.

232. (D) The only reason for any business to exist is to earn profits for the owners. Profit was therefore the primary motivation in every decision an owner made.

233. (D) An Industrial Revolution was happening in the United States at the same time as in Britain, but the two nations did not collaborate on methods.

234. (E) Owners proved very tenacious in resisting unionization, and governments were slow to realize that owners would not provide safe working conditions unless they were forced to. Industrialization began in Britain in the late 1700s, but trade unions were not legalized until 1871. The process took even longer on the Continent, with France establishing trade unions in 1884 and Germany in 1890.

235. (A) Britain had long been a wool-producing nation; this continued and expanded during the Industrial Revolution. Cotton became an important part of the industry a little later; Britain imported the raw materials from the United States and India, then spun and wove it into fabric in its own mills.

236. (D) Per capita incomes across all of industrial Europe rose to levels that people could never have imagined themselves earning in an earlier era. Even in the Balkans, Europe's least industrialized region, personal income more than doubled between 1830 and 1910.

237. (A) The accessibility of natural resources was of major importance to industrialization. Without plentiful sources of fresh water, a nation could not make use of steam power or water power for its mills and factories. Coal and timber were the other main power sources; Britain, for example, had to rely first on steam and later on coal because its timber resources were too depleted to fuel its factories.

238. (A) The railway's most important role was in shipping goods. Before the railways, overland shipping could proceed no faster than a team of horses could walk or trot. With the railways, shipping became much faster and farther. This developed new markets for goods, which meant more profit for the owners, who promptly invested their profits back into the business by expanding and hiring more workers.

239. (C) Unions were important to workers because individually, they had no leverage against an unfair owner; together, they were much stronger than the owner. Unions made possible the strike, which remains a worker's most effective weapon in negotiation with management.

240. (B) Bentham and Mill's point of view is often summed up in the phrase "the greatest good of the greatest number." They encouraged cordial relations between workers and owners by pointing out that all belonged to the same community, and the welfare of all depended on the company making a profit. Therefore what benefited one person in the community benefited all; what harmed one person made all the others that much worse off.

241. (C) Both Austria and Russia emancipated their serfs, the former in 1848, the latter in 1860.

242. (B) The liberals had gone abroad to fight in the Napoleonic Wars and had come home full of enthusiasm for Western-style constitutional government. Alexander I's attempts at reform encouraged them to hope, but when it became clear that Russia's powerful vested interests would not support liberal reforms, they rose up in rebellion.

243. (D) Serbia was well south of the border of the Austrian Empire; in fact, conflict between Austria and Serbia would later provide the spark that began World War I.

244. (B) In 1867, the Austrian Empire became the Dual Monarchy of Austria-Hungary (also called the Austro-Hungarian Empire). Francis Joseph was emperor of the dual monarchy, and it was considered one entity for financial and foreign policy, but Hungary had a separate constitution and a separate legislature.

245. (A) The nobility opposed the emancipation of the serfs, but only in the United States did a civil war ever break out over the issue of ending chattel slavery.

246. (B) Metternich was a conservative who believed in upholding and maintaining the European tradition of hereditary monarchy. Austria, along with Russia and Prussia, made up a "Holy Alliance" of nations who agreed to suppress popular insurrection wherever it arose in Europe.

247. (E) The Orthodox Church was corrupt only in the eyes of the ultra-conservative Old Believers, who had broken away from it under the early Romanov czars. The other four choices accurately describe factors that were pushing Russia toward liberalism.

248. (B) The 19th century marked the era in which Russian writers stopped imitating Western models and created a distinctly Russian literature, which in its turn shaped the literature of the West. Boris Pasternak, author of *Doctor Zhivago*, is among the greatest of Russian writers, but he belongs to a later era. Alexander Pushkin, author of the epic *Eugene Onegin*, is still considered the greatest poet in Russian history. Leo Tolstoy is best known for *War and Peace*, the towering novel of the Napoleonic Wars. Nikolai Gogol is the author of numerous satirical and comic short stories. The short novels and stories of Ivan Turgenev constitute a bridge between the Romantic era and that of the realists or Modernists.

249. (E) Choice A is wrong because there was a sharp crackdown on academic freedom in 1819; the curriculum became much more conservative. Choice B is wrong because the purpose of the Holy Alliance was to put down political insurrection wherever it occurred. Choice C is wrong because a secret state police is something that only exists under totalitarian or absolutist rule. Choice D is wrong because Alexander had indeed attempted to liberate the serfs, but he gave up in the face of stiff opposition from the conservative forces of society.

250. (A) In a common reaction to the Napoleonic Wars, Metternich believed in the principle of legitimacy—upholding and supporting the hereditary monarchies of Europe because they were the *legitimate* authorities. Conservative European leaders considered Napoleon a classic example of an illegitimate ruler—a ruler by right of conquest rather than by right of birth or even free election. Metternich was so famous for his diplomatic attempts to maintain European legitimacy that the treaties and alliances he oversaw became known as "Metternich's System."

251. (C) Francis Joseph became emperor in December 1848; in March 1849 he disbanded the popularly elected *Reichstag* and imposed a conservative, imperial "constitution" instead of adopting the liberal constitution the legislature had been about to pass.

252. (E) Despite the fact that the 19th century was a golden age of Russian literature, the writers had to work within a system of state censorship. It is all the more remarkable that they were able to publish so many works universally regarded as masterpieces.

253. (A) European victory at Vienna in 1683 had finally ended the Turks' numerous attempts to expand their empire to the north and west. The other four choices help to explain the motivations and alliances that were responsible for the outbreak and conduct of the war.

254. (A) The Decembrists were divided in their specific goals, but they all agreed that they wanted an end to absolute monarchy and the beginning of some sort of republican government.

255. (B) The Rothschilds were a very wealthy family of Austrian Jewish entrepreneurs. Rothschild money repeatedly came to the rescue of the monarchy during the Napoleonic Wars. Salomon Rothschild owned a major ironworks in the Austrian region that would later become Czechoslovakia, and Rothschild money funded the early development of the Austrian railway system.

256. (C) The Poles rebelled against Russian authority; their failure was especially unfortunate for them, as the czar instituted a brutal campaign of "Russification" against them.

257. (B) The Russian government under the czars was a true autocracy. It featured only one of the five choices listed here—a law code. Even that was not much of a guarantee to the citizens, because the czars considered themselves above the law; they revoked or ignored laws whenever they perceived the need.

258. (C) Because the Austrian Empire contained so many nationalities, nationalism acted as a divisive force. Hungarians and Italians within the empire both fought for their independence during the 19th century.

259. (A) The most important defining characteristic of Romanticism is that each work of literature or art expresses the individual personality of its creator. While the classical era had celebrated form, the Romantic era celebrated content.

260. (C) France's entire history as a republic, from 1789 through the late 19th century, demonstrates the inability of its various factions to agree on what kind of representative government they wanted.

261. (D) The German armed forces, led by the Prussians, were the best disciplined and most efficient of all the European armies of the day.

262. (E) The Labour Party did not come into existence until after World War I. The Conservative Party was formerly known as the Tory Party. Conservatives and Radicals had opposing philosophies and goals and would hardly have combined to form a new party.

263. (E) Sardinian minister Count Camillo di Cavour was the leader most responsible for Italian unification. Once Italy was formally unified, the king of Sardinia became the king of Italy, and the first Italian parliament was actually called "the eighth Sardinian parliament."

264. (C) This provision was passed several years before Gladstone took office, as part of an earlier program of reform legislation.

265. (A) The working conditions brought about by the Industrial Revolution were horrible enough to cause British workers to revolt by the thousands. One example is a weavers' demonstration at St. Peter's Field in Manchester in 1819, harshly quelled by the army and known to history as the "Peterloo Massacre" (in ironic tribute to the British victory at Waterloo).

266. (B) This is a very good description of the 19th-century liberal's ideal form of government. A Marxist or a Socialist would find it too conservative, and a conservative would prefer a hereditary monarchy with only limited legislative powers.

267. (D) Otto von Bismarck's plan was to unite Prussia and the small German-speaking states by maneuvering France into the role of their common enemy.

268. (B) Sardinia had joined the Crimean War on the French side. France returned the favor by backing Italy in the attack on Austria.

269. (D) *The Communist Manifesto* famously urges "Workers of the world, unite!" It states that the other classes—royal families, aristocrats, and the middle class—have all had their turn on top of the social and political pyramid, and it was now time for the workers to seize power. It advocates a violent revolution of the social order—not just in conservative nations, but everywhere. According to the *Manifesto*, liberal governments oppressed the working class just as much as conservative ones did.

270. (C) The issue of freedom of religion did not play a major role in the revolutions of 1848. The people were much more concerned with practical matters: safer and better working conditions in the factories, a greater say in their own government, fair wages, and reasonable prices for food and shelter. Nationalism was also a major concern; all over Europe, people attempted to assert themselves against foreign rulers and achieve self-government along ethnic-cultural-linguistic lines.

271. (E) Nationalism was a unifying force in a culturally and ethnically homogeneous country, but it was obviously a divisive force in a multi-ethnic state, especially one with large groups of ethnic minorities. Minorities in this situation wanted to break away and form their own nations. One example of this is the Hungarians in the Austrian Empire; another is the Irish under British rule.

272. (A) The pope was not only the head of the Church; he was the secular head of state of a kingdom called the Papal States, a large region of central Italy with Rome at its heart. Naturally, he was unwilling to cede his authority. In the end, the pro-unification forces were too strong for him; because Rome had been the center of a unified Italian Empire in ancient times, it had great symbolic importance to Cavour and his followers.

273. (D) Nineteenth-century Britain saw the passage of a very large number of laws that created reasonable living and working conditions for the lower classes, expanded voting rights, and made it much easier to get an education.

274. (E) For some time past, Prussia had had the mightiest army, the most efficient bureaucracy, and the strongest leadership of all the German states. Its rulers had been working and planning for unification since 1640.

275. (B) The revolutions of 1830 and 1848, and the June Days all occurred before Louis Napoleon took office as the first president of the Second Republic. The Paris Commune rose to power after Napoleon III (as he was known by this time) left office. His abrupt departure was a direct result of France's defeat in the Franco-Prussia War and the declaration of the Third Republic.

276. (E) Brahms (1833–1897) is among the best known of the German Romantic composers. "George Sand" was the pen name of novelist Amandine-Aurore-Lucille Dudevant (1804–1876), notable not only for her literary achievements but also for her habit of dressing in men's clothing, smoking cigars, and defying other rigid taboos of society. Mary Shelley (1797–1851) is best known as the author of the Romantic horror novel *Frankenstein*; like Sand, she defied traditional female roles, living openly with poet Percy Shelley before their marriage. Thus both women carried out the principle of Romanticism—expressing one's true self—in their lives as well as their writing. Verdi (1813–1901) wrote 29 operas on dramatic and historical subjects, including three based on the works of Shakespeare. Irish poet, playwright, and prose writer Yeats (1865–1939) does not belong to the Romantic era; he is considered a Modern writer.

277. (B) Without exception, the 1848 uprisings were crushed and the old regimes reasserted themselves. Apart from the abolition of serfdom in the Austrian Empire, serious reform would have to wait until the future. The overall result was that those in power before the revolutions remained in power afterward. The year 1848 can be considered a triumph of conservatism—albeit a temporary one.

278. (E) Conservatives opposed written constitutions because they didn't think they were necessary. Conservatives believed in the established institution of the monarchy. They believed in the responsibilities of the unwritten social contract—the citizens owed the monarch their service and loyalty, and the monarch owed the citizens his or her care and protection. Conservatives supported censorship because they believed that the monarch and his or her ministers were the best judges of what should be printed. According to conservative beliefs, education and the ownership of property were important indicators that a person had some stake in the government and thus was entitled to limited participation in it.

279. (A) Garibaldi was a republican and Cavour was a monarchist, but they were able to put their differences aside in their common desire for Italian unification. Garibaldi's support and that of his followers made the process of unification much swifter and easier.

280. (C) In the 19th century, liberals were those who believed in representative government—a form of government that most nations had yet to achieve. Liberals did not support hereditary monarchy because history showed that too often, the monarch turned out to be weak or incompetent. Therefore they placed their trust in a strong, popularly elected legislature that would represent the people's interests.

281. (A) *Realpolitik* is a German word meaning literally "the politics of realism"—"pragmatism" is a very close English equivalent. A pragmatic statesman is not an idealist, but someone who deals with the realities of the world as it actually exists. A pragmatist generally distrusts assurances made by other ministers, and makes choices based solely on what is in the best interest of his or her own nation. A pragmatist makes and breaks treaties, forms and breaks alliances, and gives or withdraws assurances regardless of the ethics involved—all that counts is to improve the status of his or her own nation. Other practitioners of *Realpolitik* in European history besides Bismarck include Elizabeth I of England, Cardinal Richelieu of France, and Benito Mussolini of Italy. Machiavelli's *The Prince* can be considered the bible of these hardheaded, capable, practical leaders.

282. (D) This was by no means the first time that a modern European nation had tried to pass itself off as the new Roman Empire. Byzantium had called itself "the new Rome" in the days of the emperor Constantine. In medieval times, as its name clearly indicates, the Holy Roman Empire boasted that it was the continuation of the Roman Empire. In the 1400s, after the fall of Constantinople to the Turks, Ivan III claimed that Moscow was "the Third Rome." Ivan also took the title *czar*, which like *kaiser* comes from the Latin *caesar*. Even though these empires were not geographically or culturally Italian, they wanted to associate themselves with the strength and power of the Roman Empire at its height. By calling their leader *emperor*, the Germans also recognized a kinship with the Holy Roman Empire, although in fact the former empire's ruling family governed Austria, not Germany.

283. (C) Bismarck and Cavour were both conservative. They both supported a hereditary monarchy that strongly controlled all aspects of the government. Neither put much stock in any notion of wise government by the people, or even by the people's elected representatives. Note on Choices A and B: in European history, the terms *republican* and *democrat* have no relationship to their present-day meanings in the United States. In European history, a *republican* is a person who supports representative government; a *democrat* is one who believes that all the citizens should have an equal voice in government.

284. (B) The conservative monarchies normally united to put down popular uprisings, which they believed were a serious threat to political stability. In the case of Greece they made an exception because the Greeks were rising up against rule by a Muslim nation. Europeans had regarded Muslims as heathen and inimical since the days of the Crusades, and therefore supported Christian Greece against Muslim Turkey.

285. (D) The German legislature was structurally similar to the British Parliament. It consisted of a *Bundesrat* (federal council) of hereditary nobles, whose seats passed from father to eldest son, and a *Reichstag* (imperial diet) of representatives chosen in free elections by eligible voters (at that time, all men age 25 and over). Both houses had to pass any given bill in order for it to become law.

286. (C) Conservatives are at the right of the political spectrum; therefore the least conservative, most democratic political philosophy is farthest to the left. Of the five choices, Marxism is the most democratic.

287. (B) The Greeks had won their independence from Ottoman rule in 1827 but considered themselves not yet ready for self-rule, owing to the presence of too many squabbling political factions. Therefore, the great powers of Europe suggested Prince Otto of Bavaria as the king of Greece. The forces of nationalism against a foreign ruler and liberalism against a conservative ruler caused a coup d'état in 1843; Otto conceded to most of his subjects' demands for liberal reform.

288. (A) The *Risorgimento* is the name for the drive toward unification that overcame Italy from the early years of the 19th century until the final success in 1860.

289. (B) Prussia and the other German states formed the Kingdom of Germany in 1871 in the wake of their victory over France in the Franco-Prussian War.

290. (D) The professional and mercantile middle class—the one most likely to argue for liberal reform—was far less of a political force in Spain than it was elsewhere in Western Europe. The late 19th century saw some political reform in Spain, including the passage of a written constitution, but a hereditary and highly conservative monarchy remained in place.

291. (E) Socialists and Marxists agreed on the issue of private ownership of business and industry—they both opposed it. The other four choices accurately explain why Marxism aroused opposition across the entire political spectrum of 19th-century Europe.

292. (C) The year 1848 was a great revolutionary year in Europe, shaking up a number of nation-states as various groups rose up demanding self-determination or a greater measure of democracy. Although Catholic Ireland strongly opposed British rule, Parliament passed enough reforms during the 19th century to prevent Ireland from participating in the wave of revolution that affected almost every other European nation except Russia. Note on Choice D: Italy was not yet a unified nation, but the Italian provinces in the Austrian Empire set up independent governments in 1848, and another insurrection in Rome drove the pope into temporary exile and led the people to declare a Roman Republic. In both cases the status quo was quickly reestablished.

293. (E) In Britain, women age 30 and over—if they met certain qualifications as to either property ownership or education—were first granted the right to vote in 1918. Only in 1928 were British women entitled to vote according to the same criteria as men.

294. (B) Both liberals and conservatives believed that only educated people were qualified to have a say in how they were governed. Conservatives trusted the leaders to look after the interests of the poor, because this was part of the social contract; liberals, less trustful of the leaders, argued for the regulation of industry and the formation of trade unions.

295. (A) Austria, Prussia, and Russia were among the most conservative of the European monarchies. They were in favor of maintaining the system of hereditary monarchy, and thus considered popular insurrections to be a serious threat to political stability.

Chapter 4: Empire Building and World War

296. (B) At first, China refused to barter its tea, silks, and ceramics for British goods; the Chinese insisted that they would trade only for silver. Naturally, this resulted in a vast trade surplus for China. When the British thought of importing Indian-grown opium into China, however, the trade balance was reversed almost overnight. Opium was recognized at the time as a hallucinogenic, and there was a lively market in China for illegal drugs.

297. (C) The Opium Wars are examples of "gunboat diplomacy." The treaties that ended the fighting were highly favorable to the side with the guns. Ironically, the Chinese had originally invented gunpowder, but they had not explored its use for weapons of war. This was left to the Westerners when the technology eventually found its way to Europe.

298. (B) "Indochina" refers to Vietnam, Cambodia, and Laos, which continued under French rule until the mid-20th century.

299. (C) The canal linked the Mediterranean and Red seas and was thus a shortcut alternative to the shipping lanes that had been used in the past; it cut hundreds of miles off the journey. Naturally, having financial control of the canal would be hugely profitable.

300. (E) This is the correct answer for two reasons. First, by the 19th century many of these foreign lands were no longer "unknown" to Europeans. Second, the desire to explore the unknown could perfectly well be satisfied without grabbing land, as indeed it was by many adventurous individuals. Isabella Bird, who traveled on a journey of exploration to the islands of Japan in the late 19th century, is just one example.

301. (C) Siam (present-day Thailand) was the only nation in the region that managed to maintain its independence from European rule.

302. (D) Once again, this is an example of how geography affects history. Until the Europeans came, Africa had no paved roads and no railways. Until this infrastructure was built, Europeans had no means of exploring deep into the interior in many regions; access was simply too difficult for non-natives. The climate, the forests, the insect life, and the European susceptibility to disease all proved valuable assets for the Africans, who wanted to maintain their independence.

303. (A) Together, the French and Indian War and the Seven Years' War are often referred to as "the Great War for Empire." The Franco-British conflict over India was one reason for this name.

304. (B) Libya was taken over by Italy.

305. (C) Historians estimate that Britain alone shipped more than three million Africans across the Atlantic into slavery. Italy is the only one of these five nations that played no part in the African slave trade.

306. (B) Religious missionaries did not try to organize new African governments or change the structure of the existing ones. Choices A and C accurately describe the real and practical help they brought to Africa. Choice D shows their real concern for the victims of primitive customs. Choice E shows that because their approach was humble—for example, they lived among the Africans in the same conditions as them, ate the local food, and learned to speak the native languages—their attempts to educate were received in a friendly spirit.

307. (A) There was and is no unified African culture. Africa was a continent of tribal cultures, and even neighboring tribes often spoke entirely different languages, worshiped in a different way, and made war on one another. This absence of intertribal loyalty made it relatively easy for the Europeans to recruit Africans to kidnap and sell other Africans into slavery.

308. (E) To the Europeans, Africa was a literal and figurative gold mine. Literally, it had gold and diamonds; figuratively, it had valuable crops Europeans could not raise in their own climate, such as rubber and coffee. Maize, unlike the other crops, could be (and was) grown in Europe.

309. (A) Britain, France, Russia, and Germany all established favorable trade relations with China in the wake of the Opium Wars. China would not recover its status as a major economic power until after World War II.

310. (A) The British invaders had a thoroughly racist, condescending attitude toward the conquered Indians—an attitude that the Indians found ridiculous and unjustifiable, given that the Hindus had been writing poetry and philosophy at a time when the Angles and Saxons were plundering and pillaging. It was not surprising that the sepoys (the word means "soldiers") rose up in defiance of their British commanders. The wave of uprisings was swiftly put down, in part because different segments of Indian society could not agree on what they wanted.

311. (D) In the years before World War I, the German economy was booming. This was due to industrialization and was also a by-product of unification. Now that all the small German states had become one nation, expensive trade barriers among those states had vanished overnight. All these factors helped the economy prosper.

312. (C) The Versailles Treaty addressed political rather than economic concerns.

313. (E) The newly established Communist government in Russia—soon to become the Soviet Union—viewed all Western nations as its natural enemies because they had capitalist economies. On their side, Britain and France regarded Russia's abrupt withdrawal from World War I as a betrayal, and would probably not have welcomed Lenin's participation in the peace conference.

314. (C) Ever since its defeat of the Spanish Armada, Britain had prided itself on having the finest navy in Europe, if not the world. British leaders viewed Germany's naval buildup as a direct threat to their supremacy on the seas. It also created the potential for a successful invasion of Britain, which as an island nation could only be invaded from the sea in this era that predated an attack from the air.

315. (D) The atomic bomb was not developed until World War II.

316. (A) In trench warfare, the attacking soldiers leaped out of the trenches on command and ran across open flat ground toward the enemy trenches. It was easy for the defenders to fire on them and mow them down from the safe cover of their own trenches. Defense was easy; successful attack all but impossible. Trench warfare was designed for hand-to-hand close combat, but the weapons of the day were designed to kill from a distance.

317. (C) The Bolsheviks seized power in Russia in 1917. Russian leader Vladimir Ilyich Lenin had no interest whatever in defeating the Germans or aiding Russia's French and British allies; his goal was to withdraw immediately from World War I and swiftly settle Russia's domestic affairs. Therefore Russia withdrew from combat, signing the Treaty of Brest-Litovsk with Germany in early 1918.

318. (B) The Schlieffen Plan was specifically designed to prevent the need to fight on two fronts at the same time. Since Germany was positioned geographically between two of its enemies—France and Russia—Schlieffen devised a plan that would eliminate France before attacking Russia.

319. (B) When Russia mobilized against Austria in 1914, Germany declared war on Russia. France and Britain supported Russia because the three nations had signed a series of formal alliances between 1894 and 1907. The United States and Italy did not join the fight until later.

320. (C) Germany interpreted Russian mobilization against Austria as the obvious prelude to a declaration of war, and came to Austria's defense immediately by declaring war on Russia.

321. (C) Serbia had hoped for a formal union with Bosnia-Herzegovina, since the two nations were culturally linked. Austria's annexation of Bosnia prevented this, arousing fierce resentment among Serbian nationalists, of whom Gavrilo Princip was an extreme example.

322. (E) The Schlieffen Plan had called for the German army to march west through Belgium into France, then turn south and march directly on Paris. In fact, the Germans turned south much too early, and met the French forces on the Marne River, which was well to the east of Paris. The unexpected French victory marked the failure of the Schlieffen Plan and the beginning of the long war of attrition on the Western Front.

323. (D) Allied troops would occupy Germany after World War II, but this did not happen in the wake of World War I.

324. (B) The idea behind the League of Nations was that it would protect large and small nations on an equal basis. When nations came into conflict, leaders would discuss and try to resolve the situation around the conference table, with war being only a last resort. Leaders also agreed that if one nation attacked another, all the other nations would unite in defense of the attacked nation.

325. (D) The Social Democrats would soon lose their majority in the *Reichstag*; they would form a series of short-lived coalition governments until the Nazis took control in the early 1930s.

326. (B) The entry of fresh troops on the Western Front was the decisive factor in the German defeat.

327. (E) The Tannenberg campaign was a series of battles fought on the Eastern Front. This early German victory made the Germans reverse their earlier belief that it would be easy to win on the Western Front, difficult on the Eastern Front.

328. (B) Air attacks, bombs, and large-scale explosives did not play nearly as large a role in World War I as they would play in later wars. Therefore there was minimal destruction in the cities and large towns; the battlefields of the war were generally far from any urban centers.

329. (D) Ironically, given the fact that President Woodrow Wilson suggested the League of Nations, the United States did not become a member. The U.S. Congress, not wishing to commit to foreign wars except on a case-by-case basis, voted against joining the League.

330. (A) The concept of nationalism had gained widespread acceptance and belief during the 19th century. The leaders at Versailles therefore tried to redraw the map so that the people within each nation would be culturally, linguistically, and ethnically homogeneous. This lessened the possibility that ethnic minorities would rise up against their governments, thus helping to preserve peace everywhere. The balance of power was another major motivating factor, particularly in the granting of independence to Poland and the breakup of the Austro-Hungarian Empire.

331. (D) Germany was left to establish its own government after the war ended. This would not be the case after World War II, when the Allied forces worked directly with the Germans to rebuild their government from the ground up.

332. (A) The Balkan League, an association among the small nations of southeastern Europe, was formed in 1912, before the Balkan Wars. The region underwent a period of political unrest both before and during the wars; examples include the suspension of Croatia's constitution in 1912, a series of regime changes in Hungary, and major land grabs by Serbia.

333. (C) The serfs were emancipated in 1860; this had happened too far in the past to be considered a contributing cause of the 1905 Revolution. At best, it was an indirect cause. Emancipation led to a major controversy over how best to provide the peasants with land of their own, and in its turn land ownership was a major issue in the insurrection.

334. (A) Russia had continued to expand eastward, reaching the Sea of Japan by 1860 and establishing the port city of Vladivostok. By 1904, the Trans-Siberian Railroad connected Vladivostok with the west. In 1900, Russian troops occupied Manchuria; Japan considered this a serious military threat to its own security and acted accordingly.

335. (C) With the Austrian annexation of Bosnia-Herzegovina in 1908, Russia was forced to acknowledge that it had failed in its long-term goal of domination in the Black Sea and the Balkans. Russia had assumed it would take the place of the Ottoman Empire as the dominant power in this largely Slavic and Eastern Orthodox region. However, Russia's severe social, political, and economic problems got in the way of its territorial ambitions. Note on Choice E: Russia was like all the other European nations in trusting the men who had led it to victory in various 19th-century conflicts. These men assumed that a 20th-century war would be no different from what they were used to; they did not grasp that technology had continued to advance and that new weapons called for new strategies. The blithe assumption that war was a local, quickly won affair was soon proved a tragic mistake.

336. (B) The Poles defeated the Bolsheviks on the battlefield and both sides signed the Treaty of Riga in 1921. It established a new Russian-Polish border that would last until the Soviet invasion of Poland in 1939.

337. (B) On October 17, Czar Nicholas II offered the people a compromise known as the October Manifesto. It offered near-universal voting rights (for men) and other civil and religious liberties. It permitted workers to organize unions and voters to form political parties for the first time in Russian history. It also held out the promise of an elected legislature. The October Manifesto had the effect of dividing the opposition and winning the support of the more moderate factions. In the following weeks, leaders of the Petrograd Soviet were arrested; uprisings of the lower classes would continue for many months, but in the end the monarchy was able to maintain a tenuous control.

338. (A) Lenin recognized that Russia must maintain trade relations with other nations that had capitalist or mixed economies, but he would never have dreamed of any sort of private enterprise within Russia itself.

339. (E) Czar Nicholas II abdicated in favor of the Provisional Government, which consisted of former members of the *Duma* (the Russian parliament) who represented a coalition of political parties. The Provisional Government, as its name suggests, was not intended as a permanent solution to Russia's future after the monarchy was abolished. Its purpose was to write a constitution and establish a new permanent government. As the weeks and months went by, it became clear that the Provisional Government was too divided, too conservative, and too weak to carry out its tasks.

340. (D) Russia suffered a humiliating and financially costly military defeat at the hands of the Japanese. The war permanently defined the eastern borders of the Russian—later Soviet—empire. Japan's goal had been to put a stop to Russian expansion into China.

341. (C) A *soviet* is a workers' council. Workers' councils had played a major role in the 1905 Revolution. After the February 1917 uprising, the Petrograd Soviet would rise to a position of authority as it became clear that the Provisional Government could not control the country's political and social turmoil.

342. (D) The Russian army was larger than the German one, but that was its only advantage at this period of history. It was disorganized, poorly disciplined, and armed with weapons inferior to those of the Germans. By the time World War II broke out, this situation would change.

343. (A) Eager to get out of World War I as quickly as possible, even on less than ideal terms, Lenin ceded a vast swath of Russia's western territory to Germany.

344. (C) Since Lenin intended to make Russia into a workers' state, the workers naturally supported Lenin's side—the Reds—in the civil war.

345. (E) The White Army, not the Red Army, is the one that relied in part on foreign troops.

346. (A) There were tens of thousands of Socialists in Europe, but they were generally able to find a place in the parliamentary governments of the western nations. In the 19th century, Western European workers had gained many important concessions, such as voting rights and trade-union membership. Therefore, the Bolshevik example did not inspire European rebellion except on a small scale.

347. (E) The New Economic Policy required all peasants to sell their surplus grain to the state; it would be used to feed the urban industrial workers.

348. (B) At Versailles, Germany was made to surrender all the territory it had acquired during the war. If Russian leaders had been present, they might have made a good case that Russia was entitled to take back at least some of the territory, such as the Ukraine.

349. (D) The Five-Year Plan was an economic program, not a political one. Stalin did indeed eliminate freedom of speech and of the press, but this was a political act, not part of an economic policy.

350. (B) In old Russia, the czar and the Orthodox Church had been the two great authorities—indeed, they were connected, because the people believed that the czar ruled by divine right. In the newly renamed Soviet Union, the dictator did not permit any rival authority. Officially, the Soviet Union was an atheist state.

351. (D) Previous revolutions had been confined to the state in which they took place. Revolutions often involved civil war, a change in the form of government, the rise to power of a dictator, and/or equality among social ranks, but never before had a revolution been intended to overturn the entire existing social order across several nations.

352. (A) The Soviet Union had only one political party, the Communist Party (the Bolshevik Party under a new name). Lenin was the absolute dictator; his authority could not be questioned.

353. (B) Stalin was brutal to all his subjects, but the farmers came in for his greatest contempt and disdain. Stalin considered both peasants and independent farmers nothing more than a means of providing grain to feed the workers—farmers, to him, did not count as workers because they worked in agriculture rather than the heavy industry that he considered the key to economic prosperity.

354. (D) Lenin insisted on ruling Russia (soon to become the Soviet Union) as sole dictator, without the assistance or interference of a legislature. His observation of Western European governments had convinced him that parliaments were mere tools of the capitalist forces of society—business owners, wealthy merchants, and managers.

355. (C) The rise of a Communist state in Hungary, under Bela Kun, lasted five months and is known as the "Red Terror." It was replaced by a less repressive government under the naval commander and former diplomat Miklos Horthy.

356. (E) Germany was in no condition to stockpile arms and ammunition during the 1920s. It had many other serious concerns: political, economic, and social. Starting another war of aggression was the last thing on the minds of the German leaders until Hitler rose to power.

357. (A) The purpose of the Treaty of Trianon, signed by Hungary and most of the World War I Allied nations, was to create an autonomous state of Hungary along ethnic lines. This meant redrawing Hungary's borders and making smaller ethnic states, such as Czechoslovakia, of some of its territory. Like many of the attempts to redraw the European map after World War I, the Treaty of Trianon was decidedly mixed in its effects. Hungary lost more than 70 percent of its territory and more than 60 percent of its people—many of whom were ethnically, culturally, and linguistically Hungarian.

358. (D) The ripple effects of the Great Depression affected all of Europe, including Poland. By the mid-1930s the Polish economy was shifting more and more toward nationalization; in addition, government controls over other aspects of society tightened and the president's powers were extended. Still, the government remained authoritarian and militaristic without being Fascist; Poles managed to retain certain important civil and individual rights in the period before World War II.

359. (B) Italy gained territory from Austria after World War I. The other four answer choices describe a general climate of economic and social unrest in Italy that most Italians blamed on the workers. Italians called their leaders cowards for supporting the Socialists; they felt that the workers were undermining the whole fabric of society and creating a climate of fear. When the Fascists began their terrorist tactics against the Socialists, most Italians applauded them for having more courage than the legitimate government.

360. (E) When a state adopts a policy of autarky, it proclaims its ability to take care of all the needs of its people without importing any goods from other nations. This was tried in Germany and Italy under Hitler and Mussolini, and later in Spain and Poland.

361. (B) Hitler took the simplest possible means to his goal of presiding over a politically unified Nazi Party. His own inclinations were conservative, partly because he was afraid the radical Nazis might support some leader other than himself, partly because he wanted the support of key conservative elements—the army, the foreign office, and the treasury. On June 30, 1934—the Night of the Long Knives—the SS murdered several of the radical Nazi leaders, thus effectively quashing any division within Hitler's following.

362. (C) Dollfuss disbanded the Austrian parliament and established himself as a dictator immediately after Hitler became chancellor of Germany. Because the Social Democrats were the party most prone to argue for reform, to support workers' strikes, and to protest against the establishment, Dollfuss considered them to be a divisive and destabilizing force in society at a time of real peril—a greater threat than the rise of the Nazis in Germany. Dollfuss himself represented the Christian Socials, and it was the Christian Social agenda that he imposed on Austria. After an uprising and a brief exchange of gunshots in Vienna, the Social Democratic Party was made illegal and many of its leaders went into exile.

363. (B) Some of the key factors that contributed to the success of Fascism elsewhere in Europe did not exist in France. France was badly hit by the Great Depression, but because its economy depended less on heavy industry than did those of Germany and Britain, the impact was less severe. No strong Fascist leader emerged in France; this was always a requisite for the rise of a lasting Fascist regime. France also had a strong tradition of individual rights and republicanism that mitigated against Fascism. Worker demonstrations in Italy and Austria contributed largely to the rise of totalitarian governments there; in France, by contrast, the conservative establishment did not perceive the political left as an active threat that must be suppressed. France's internal political decisions in the 1930s had nothing to do with its foreign alliances.

364. (D) Daily wage laborers formed the backbone of the Socialist and Communist organizations in Italy as elsewhere. The Fascists opposed any notion of the workers' rise to power; they considered themselves the workers' victims. For example, civil servants had seen their salaries drop drastically during the worker uprisings of 1919 and 1920, and blamed it on the Socialist uprisings (although in fact the causes of Italy's economic troubles were much more complex).

365. (C) The Nazis did not eliminate religious worship in Germany. In 1933, Germany signed a concordat with the Church that permitted it to continue to fulfill its religious role in exchange for its elimination as a force in German politics.

366. (A) Austrian leaders had been considering a customs union with Germany for some time; many Austrian factions were agitating for a full political union (which would in fact come to pass with the *Anschluss*). The Nazi Party had become a force in Austrian politics by this time, just as it had risen to power in Germany. The League of Nations viewed this with serious concern, and insisted that if it loaned Austria the money it so desperately needed to stave off total economic collapse, Austria must promise to drop any idea of Austro-German union, even if only in the matter of trade.

367. (C) The Spanish government that came to power in 1939 was a Fascist dictatorship led by General Francisco Franco.

368. (A) Choices B through D are false statements because the Nazi and Fascist regimes were both characterized by all four descriptions. Choice A reveals a crucial difference between Nazi Germany and Fascist Italy. Mussolini's hold on power was tenuous compared to Hitler's. Mussolini was only the prime minister; Italy still had a king who had the right to dismiss him at any time. Italy had an entrenched political, military, and bureaucratic establishment that Mussolini preferred to pacify and assimilate into his own power structure; in Germany, Hitler simply purged all these elements of the administrative structure and replaced them with his own most loyal and committed followers.

369. (C) The prosperous middle class is historically on the side of Fascism rather than Communism; the middle class is much more likely to side with the wealthy ranks of society than with the workers.

370. (A) Historians agree unanimously that the leaders at Versailles made a tragic mistake in insisting on Germany's total humiliation. Ordinary Germans deeply resented their own government for accepting the situation; the Nazis cashed in on the people's discontentment by showing that they were a strong, military party that was ripe for reclaiming German honor.

371. (D) The war had been so devastating in terms of loss of life and hardship on the home front that no one wanted to go through it again. Leaders had their doubts about Hitler and his intentions, but anyone who had publicly supported war would swiftly have been voted out of office.

372. (C) In the Lateran Treaty, Benito Mussolini granted the Catholic Church extensive control over the everyday lives of the Italian people (for example, the Church controlled the Italian school system and censored the film industry) in exchange for the pope's official recognition of the Republic of Italy. Like Napoleon, Mussolini was not religiously devout; ecclesiastical recognition was very important for the legitimacy of the Italian state, and Mussolini considered that the power he was asked to grant the Church in return was a small price to pay.

373. (C) Germany no doubt resented the role the United States had played in World War I, but in most of the other nations where Fascism rose up, American participation in the war was not a factor. The other four choices accurately describe social, economic, and political problems that allowed ultra-right-wing governments to rise to power.

374. (A) Germany was unable to pay the reparations in the agreed amount, because the money simply was not there; France refused to accept this fact, and marched into the Ruhr to take their money's worth of coal.

375. (C) The Socialists had supported public ownership of land; naturally the landowners opposed this, preferring to hold onto their private property. The Fascists were anti-Socialist on principle, and it was easy for them to gain the landowners' support by openly saying so.

376. (A) The king was afraid of the Blackshirts, who had proved themselves to be terrorists. He felt that it was better to come to terms with them peaceably than to open fire on them.

377. (E) The youth groups for boys and girls were made compulsory as of December 1936. They were a way to indoctrinate children into the one-party Nazi system. The hikes and sporting activities were no doubt enjoyable for many of the children, but the state's purpose was to build a physically strong future Germany. Not surprisingly, the Nazis did not want German children exposed to other systems of government or non-German ways of thinking.

378. (A) The Catholics, being conservative, did not support the Popular Front, which included Communists, Socialists, and radicals.

379. (A) As of 1920, Hungary was ruled by the authoritarian (although not Fascist) government of Miklos Horthy. From 1926 to 1935, Jósef Pilsudski's authoritarian, sometimes dictatorial regime ruled Poland; after Pilsudski's death, the military held most of the power until the combined Nazi-Soviet invasion. Romania between the world wars was a violent, turbulent absolutist state under King Carol II (who twice went into exile). Yugoslavia was also a royal dictatorship from 1929 until the Nazi invasion of 1941. Czechoslovakia, by contrast, managed to establish and maintain a representative government.

380. (B) No dictator can survive without the support of the men with the guns. Guns are the most powerful of all possible deterrents to opposition, be it political opposition or any other kind.

381. (D) The Conservatives called for a vote of censure against MacDonald when he loaned money to the Soviet Union. In response, MacDonald called for an election; he was overwhelmingly defeated. Britain had not forgiven the Soviets for abandoning the fight in 1917.

382. (A) France's greatest fear was another German invasion; the French government built up the military and also ordered the construction of the Maginot Line.

383. (D) Igor Stravinsky was an expatriate Soviet composer who settled in France, where he wrote the notorious *Rite of Spring* ballet in the year before World War I broke out. The other four are all Germans who were internationally recognized for their contributions to painting, musical theater, poetry, drama, and the cinema. Brecht, Weill, and Von Sternberg all emigrated to the United States in the wake of Hitler's rise to power.

384. (C) Bitterness over the defeat in the war existed independently of the indecisiveness of the German political leaders. The other four choices are all direct results of their ineffective leadership.

385. (E) The Popular Front won a decisive majority of the seats in the Cortés (the Spanish legislative assembly) and brought Manuel Azaña back into power as prime minister.

386. (A) With no experience in governing, Hitler never outlined any specific social or foreign-policy programs. In his view, the people should not be given any opportunity to pass judgment on such things anyway; they should simply take it on trust that their leader would provide for them.

387. (D) Mussolini was far from a failure before he became *Il Duce*; he was a well-educated man, a serious reader, and an experienced journalist.

388. (B) Choices A and D are wrong because they are false statements. Choices C and E are wrong because they had little, if anything, to do with political leaders' dismissal of Hitler as a serious political threat. The establishment focused mainly on Hitler's lack of experience and the fact that he did not campaign according to traditional rules.

389. (D) Communism and Fascism are both synonymous with totalitarianism. Choices A, B, C, and E are all demonstrated in the histories of the Fascist and Communist governments of Europe in the 20th century. Governments in both Nazi Germany and Fascist Italy, however, brought economic prosperity, at least in the short term.

390. (D) Hitler did not rise to power until after 1930 and was in no sense responsible for the German economic recovery of 1922. He was certainly responsible for the economic recovery of the 1930s.

391. (C) The opposite of this statement is true; the Allied powers vastly outnumbered the German and Italian forces. The Soviet Union alone sent more troops into battle than most of the other nations combined.

392. (E) The Potsdam Declaration, issued in the wake of the conference, states that Allied forces—not solely U.S. forces—would occupy Japan from the time of surrender until the Allies were satisfied that the terms of surrender had been met. The American army played the leading role in the occupation, and was headed by American General Douglas MacArthur, but Australian, British, and Indian troops also took part.

393. (C) Since Hitler and Stalin had signed a nonaggression pact, the German invasion came as a complete surprise to the Soviets; however, they immediately rallied against the Nazis, joining the war on the Allied side.

394. (E) The Allied commanders agreed that the Americans would join the British forces fighting General Rommel's troops in North Africa. According to plan, they defeated Rommel, then moved into the Italian islands and thence into mainland Italy.

395. (E) The Soviet Union alone lost more troops and more civilians than all the other nations combined.

396. (A) General Eisenhower deliberately allowed the Germans to intercept false and misleading messages about the planned invasion. The Germans believed these messages were genuine; therefore they expected the invasion to take place many miles farther along the French coast, and thus they did not protect the Normandy beaches where the Allies actually landed.

397. (E) In 1919, the Versailles Treaty had awarded the Danzig Corridor to Poland. This 50-mile-wide swath of land lay geographically between East Prussia and the rest of Germany. Hitler's goal was to retake this territory and thus reunite all of Germany into one landmass.

398. **(A)** In 1940, Marshall Pétain was second in command in the French government. He seized power, arranging an armistice with the Nazis after the German invasion. Pétain immediately became the titular head of the Vichy government (named for the city in southern central France where it took up its headquarters). Partly from genuine political conviction and partly to stave off further German invasions, Pétain shaped Vichy France into an authoritarian, right-wing state that echoed many of the political and social policies of Fascist Italy and Nazi Germany.

399. **(B)** The purpose of the Maginot Line was to serve as a defensive barrier to protect France from a potential German invasion.

400. **(B)** Hitler's irrational belief that Slavs were *Untermenschen*—meaning literally "subhuman"—led him to assume Germany would win a quick and easy victory over the Soviet Union. This was only one of his many serious strategic errors. Germany inflicted a great deal of damage and loss on the USSR, but was fatally weakened in its turn by having to expend so much manpower and effort on the Eastern Front.

401. **(A)** Hitler dreamed of a Thousand-Year Reich that would dominate Europe. Choice B is wrong because his original intention toward Britain was friendly. Choice C is wrong because this policy did not take shape until the early 1940s. Choice D is wrong because Hitler saw the Soviet Union as a political enemy and a nation of *Untermenschen* that it was Germany's mission to conquer. Choice E is wrong because Hitler never intended to fight simultaneous wars on two fronts; he assumed that the Germans could quickly win on one front, then turn all their attention to the other.

402. **(E)** The French Resistance was the armed, organized popular protest movement against the Vichy regime and the Nazi occupying forces. As the war dragged on, the Resistance gained more and more popular support among French civilians. Running a black market would have been entirely against everything the Resistance stood for; black marketeers are those who try to make financial profits from the misfortunes and deprivations of the civilian population during wartime.

403. **(D)** These dates are all important milestones in the war, but "D-Day" specifically refers to the landing on the Normandy beaches. This event spelled certain defeat for Germany.

404. **(D)** When the German troops marched into France, the outnumbered and outgunned Allies were forced to retreat north across the English Channel. The result was that Germany immediately subdued the northern half of France, which it would continue to occupy until 1944. Although the British still speak of Dunkirk with pride because of the number of people they rescued, it was nonetheless a military defeat.

405. **(C)** Germany occupied the Rhineland in 1936. Hitler annexed Austria in 1938 in an event the Germans called the *Anschluss*, or "union." The Germans marched into Czechoslovakia between October 1938 and March 1939. Immediately after the German invasion of Poland in September 1939, Britain and France declared war on Germany. In May 1940, the Germans invaded France; they controlled it within a matter of weeks.

406. (E) The Soviet Union had no involvement in European foreign affairs in 1938. Stalin would take no hand in the game until he and Hitler signed a nonaggression pact in August 1939.

407. (C) France began the war as Choice A, a combatant on the Allied side against Nazi Germany, but signed an armistice with Germany in June 1940. From then until the liberation of Paris in August 1944, France was occupied by the Nazi army. Northern France was under direct military rule by the Germans; southern France had a right-wing French government, known as the Vichy regime, that was under Germany's sway.

408. (D) The farther the German troops penetrated into the Soviet Union, the farther they were getting from their own sources of supply. Napoleon and the Grand Army had made the same mistake in 1812. Again like Napoleon, Hitler failed to realize how severely a Russian winter would affect troops who came from a milder climate. Each casualty was a much greater loss to Germany than to the Soviet Union, because the Soviets had a much larger pool of reinforcements from which to draw and those reinforcements had a much shorter distance to travel to the front lines.

409. (A) The attack on France was a swift success, therefore not a strategic error. The declaration of war on the United States made an enemy of a powerful nation. The invasion of the Soviet Union similarly made an enemy of the largest and fiercest army in Europe. The annexation of so much Eastern European territory spread German resources far too thin. The belief that Britain and France would not interfere with Germany's eastward expansion led Hitler to invade Poland, which immediately provoked Britain and France to declare war on Germany.

410. (C) The tide of popular opinion in Italy had generally turned against Mussolini by 1943, and the Italians looked on the invading Allied troops as a rescue force. Italy joined the Allied side and Italian troops participated in the liberation of major cities in the north. Mussolini, imprisoned by the king immediately after the invasion, escaped and was aided by the Germans. In the end, the Italian Resistance murdered him.

411. (E) The Battle of Britain was fought between the German Luftwaffe and the British air force (supplemented by a large number of Polish pilots) and the civilians. The Germans' purpose was to destroy the British fighting spirit and ruin British morale by bombing London and other areas heavily populated by civilians. The British response, however, was just the opposite—they rose to the occasion by banding together in defiance of the Germans. British and Polish airmen destroyed so many German planes that the Luftwaffe eventually gave up the bombing campaign as too costly.

412. (B) Unemployment dropped to near-zero levels during the war. The reason was simple. Millions of men were employed by the armed forces; this left their civilian jobs to be filled by women. Throughout Europe, women took over traditionally male jobs—as taxi drivers, auto mechanics, mail carriers, train conductors, crane operators, and factory foremen. The munitions industry necessary to total war created millions of jobs throughout Europe. The spying described in Choice E was the inevitable result of living under totalitarian rule; dictators believed that if neighbors spied on one another, everyone would be too frightened to speak out against authority or to incite any kind of protest or rebellion.

413. (B) The European leaders met at Munich in 1938 to work out the future of Czechoslovakia. In the end, they agreed that Germany, Hungary, and Poland would each take over particular sections of Czechoslovakia, with Italy and Germany pledging to guarantee the sovereignty of the remainder.

414. (A) The bombings did maintain a constant level of terror that was very hard to bear—people in large cities such as London and later Berlin were constantly braced for the ear-splitting air-raid alarms—but this proved a unifying rather than a divisive force. Everyone in the city was equally in danger from the bombing; therefore it created a bond.

415. (B) As the fighting wore on, much of the German elite, including high-ranking members of the Nazi Party, grew more and more dissatisfied with Hitler's policies. (They had good reason; historians agree that during the last years of the war, Hitler was no longer entirely sane.) These men formed the goal of creating a new, powerful German Reich, but without Hitler and without the worst aspects of Nazism. The assassination attempt failed and a large number of suspects were summarily executed.

416. (B) The *Anschluss*, or "union," was Hitler's term for the German annexation of Austria. Austria was literally absorbed into Germany and would not exist again as an independent nation until after the war ended.

417. (E) Hitler's main motive for the invasion was to expand German territory—his overall aim was to create a vast German empire in central and eastern Europe. By invading the Soviet Union, he would preempt any possible Soviet attempt to take over territory that Hitler himself intended to conquer for the Reich. Despite the political similarity between Fascism and Communism in practice, the two philosophies were theoretically opposed; Hitler loathed Communism and was pleased to attack a Communist nation. Hitler was aware of the Stalinist purges and the terrible losses Russia had suffered during World War I; this knowledge, along with his racist prejudice against Slavs, caused him to underestimate the fierceness of the Soviet military response.

418. (C) To get to the Mediterranean or the Western Front, U.S. troops had only to board ships and cross the Atlantic Ocean. The Eastern Front, on the other hand, was geographically all but inaccessible from the West, because so much Axis-controlled territory lay between. The fuel, transport, food, supplies, and human energy that would have been consumed moving thousands of troops across the entire continent of Europe made it out of the question for the U.S. troops to come to the rescue of their Soviet allies until at least some of the intervening obstacles had been removed. Stalin, of course, believed that the Allies were quite content to leave the struggle to Soviet troops as long as possible—and historians agree that there is at least some justification for this view.

419. (A) "Peace in our time" was a highly overoptimistic assessment of the Munich agreements. Europe would be engaged in all-out war within eight months of the Munich conference.

420. (A) The Germans invaded Norway in April 1940 and installed a puppet government, thus making Norway part of Axis Europe. Fascist Spain contributed troops to various Axis attacks in the east at the beginning of the war, but remained officially neutral throughout the war.

421. (D) Mussolini expanded Italian territory into Greece, Yugoslavia, Albania, and Libya.

422. (A) The Germans did not even try to attack the Maginot Line where it was strongest, along the German/French border. Instead, they invaded France through the Netherlands and Belgium, north of the main strength of the Maginot Line.

423. (B) Stalin wanted Hitler's assurance that there would be no German attempt to stop the USSR from annexing the Baltic republics of Estonia, Latvia, and Lithuania. He was also receptive to Hitler's suggestion that Germany and the Soviet Union divide Poland between them.

424. (E) The Soviets made good on Stalin's promise, joining in the war in the Pacific after Berlin fell to the Allies. The war in the Pacific ended with the Japanese surrender in September 1945.

425. (E) The United States did not send troops to Europe until after it formally entered the war in 1941.

426. (C) Choice C is true only of Soviet-controlled Poland; the Soviets had outlawed religious worship in their own country, so naturally they banned it in conquered territory. Under the Nazis, most Catholic parishes in western Poland continued to function, albeit under severe restrictions.

427. (A) Spain maintained official neutrality during the war, but did not sit idly by and watch its progress without taking any hand in the game. Franco supported Hitler's invasion of the Soviet Union, but opposed his persecution of the Jews, and acted accordingly on both issues. Both Axis and Allied leaders hoped that Spain would join the fight on their side. Knowing that both sides were likely to turn their backs on Spain after the war, Franco early began preparing Spain for autarky (economic self-sufficiency).

Chapter 5: The Cold War and the Fall of Communism

428. (B) During the process of British withdrawal, the leaders in India agreed to form two separate states—a culturally Hindu India and a culturally Muslim Pakistan. At that time, Pakistan was two large, geographically separate regions at the northeastern and northwestern corners of the subcontinent; the northeastern corner would become the independent nation of Bangladesh in 1971.

429. (C) After the German invasions of Russia/Soviet Union in both world wars—particularly the 1941 invasion, which was a betrayal of a signed agreement—Stalin was convinced that the USSR required a buffer zone to protect it from the West.

430. **(C)** To ease the transition to African independence after World War II, British officials in the colonies encouraged Africans to attend school and to take responsible jobs in the police, the bureaucracy, and industry. The result was that when independence came, Africans in British colonies such as Ghana had the necessary experience and education to take charge of their own countries. This happened to a much greater extent in the African nations colonized by Britain than in those colonized by other European powers.

431. **(B)** During World War II, life as Eastern Europeans knew it was completely swept away and replaced by a whole new set of conditions. Because of the national emergency, people became accustomed to government regulation. This created an atmosphere highly favorable to the rise of Communist rule—it was very similar to a wartime economy in its tight regulation of all aspects of business and industry. Direct experience of the Red Army, however, made many look on Communism with grave fears.

432. **(C)** The Communist system of government guarantees everyone a job. Choice A is wrong because Communists believe in state censorship of the press and the arts. Choice B is wrong because housing was generally cramped and poor-quality. Choice D is true in theory but totally false in practice; Party members—particularly high officials—enjoyed many luxuries and comforts denied to the ordinary people. Choice E is wrong because the state kept wages low.

433. **(D)** Communists were in a position of such power in Eastern Europe after 1945 that they had no need to hide their identities. It would have been impossible for them even had they wished to, since the entire world knew perfectly well that all Soviets were Communists.

434. **(E)** Gomulka had been appointed deputy prime minister in 1948, but he advocated a milder and more gradual implementation of Socialism than the hard-line Communism practiced by Stalin. Imprisoned in 1951, Gomulka was released in 1954 during the post-Stalinist thaw. As the authorities hastily discussed how to combat the uprising, Gomulka appeared the obvious compromise choice—popular among his own people because he was a Pole and a symbol of Stalinist repression, but tolerated by the Communists because he was a committed Socialist. After a forceful speech against the worst excesses of Stalinism, Gomulka was chosen as First Secretary of the Politburo—in effect, the head of the Polish government.

435. **(B)** Westerners visiting East Berlin was not the primary concern of the East German and Soviet leaders; west-to-east travel was permitted throughout the Cold War, although it was hampered with irksome restrictions until the Quadripartite Pact of 1971. They built the Berlin Wall to stop the east-to-west flow of emigration, having realized how bad it looked for their system that their best and brightest people—university-educated scholars, trained engineers and scientists, and creative artists—were leaving in droves. Of course, it did not look much better to have to build a wall to keep their people from leaving them, as President John F. Kennedy observed in a famous speech he made in West Berlin.

436. (E) The Soviet Union installed nuclear missiles in Cuba, its ally and fellow Communist nation, in 1961. United States reconnaissance planes spotted and photographed the missiles, and a tense standoff began between the two superpowers. President Kennedy decided to respond with a naval blockade of Cuba. At the last moment, as Soviet ships bore down on the blockade, Khrushchev ordered them to turn back. This was the closest the world had come to an all-out nuclear war since the U.S. bombing of Japan in 1945.

437. (D) The Prague Spring was a brief era of reform that began in 1968 when Dubcek took office. He rolled back censorship and granted real powers to the legislature. Within the year, the Soviets sent troops into Czechoslovakia to remove Dubcek from office and overturn his reforms. In 2011, the Prague Spring gave its name to the "Arab Spring," a wave of popular uprisings in Egypt, Libya, Tunisia, and elsewhere.

438. (E) Yugoslavian leader Josip Broz Tito expelled the last of the Soviet troops and officials from the country in 1948. The Soviets retaliated by throwing Tito out of the Comintern. Under his rule, Yugoslavia achieved a mixed economy, with elements of both Socialism and capitalism.

439. (C) Britain, the USSR, and the United States were considered the major players on the Allied side. When France protested at being overlooked, it was included among the occupying nations.

440. (A) The Soviets had backed Congolese nationalist Patrice Lumumba in his rise to power; U.S. leaders erroneously assessed Lumumba as a Soviet puppet, and therefore backed the factions opposed to him. Although Belgium has admitted its own role in Lumumba's assassination, the part played in it by the United States is still an unsolved question. Violent regime changes and a brutal civil war among the various factions followed. The Congo has known very little political stability down to the present day.

441. (E) The most important duty of the Allies, as they saw it in 1945, was to obliterate any remnants of the Nazi Party and its political philosophy. Other motives included working with the Germans to install a new bureaucracy; to rebuild their economy and infrastructure; to set up a new, democratic government; and to rebuild institutions such as the school system, the police, and the courts.

442. (C) Churchill first used this term in a speech he gave during a 1946 visit to the United States. He warned that "an iron curtain has descended across the continent" of Europe, and that all the nations behind this imaginary border were subject to "a very high . . . measure of control from Moscow." In the months and years after the speech, the imaginary Iron Curtain became solid and real as a series of border fences and walls were erected, most notably the barrier surrounding West Berlin.

443. (A) The Lateran Treaty of 1929 had determined the Church's role in Italian society. The other four choices describe issues that the Italian leaders were left to solve on their own. Germany was occupied by the former Allied nations and had its government and economy completely overhauled under Allied supervision, but Italy, as an Allied nation, was left to decide its own future.

444. (B) Since 1945, Western Europe has been characterized by a spirit of international alliances such as NATO, the Common Market, and the European Union. After the massive destruction of the war, European leaders realized that their nations were stronger together than when they stood on their own and fought among themselves. Note on Choice D: this is the wrong answer because it is not true of Western Europe across the board; it applies only to those nations where Fascism or Nazism had taken hold and had to be rooted out and replaced.

445. (D) The European Recovery Plan is universally referred to as the Marshall Plan in honor of the man who created it. As a result of the Marshall Plan, the United States provided outright financial gifts to Western Europe in the amount of $13 billion. The aid was offered to all the nations of Europe with the sole exception of Spain, which was still under the authoritarian rule of Francisco Franco. (Spain was also excluded from the United Nations.) Stalin blocked all nations under Soviet sway from accepting. He considered it a blatant American attempt to purchase goodwill.

446. (A) Membership in NATO as of 1949 included several Western European nations plus the United States and Canada. NATO was an agreement made for the purposes of mutual security and defense. Each member nation of NATO agreed to rise to the defense of any other member nation that was invaded or attacked.

447. (B) Khrushchev startled the world by giving an unscheduled, four-hour speech at the Congress in which he described and denounced many of the worst aspects of Stalin's brutal repressions. This was part and parcel of a general Soviet process of "de-Stalinization"—in other words, smashing the cult of personality that Stalin had carefully cultivated to make himself a mythic, superhuman figure throughout the nation. However, de-Stalinization did not mean the abandonment of one-party Communist rule. This would not happen for another 40 years.

448. (D) A Communist economy and a capitalist economy are inherently opposed to one another. Stalin believed that his Western allies would never permit Germany to make a free choice between Communism and capitalism.

449. (B) Military invasions into both nations swept the reforming leader out of office and replaced him with a Soviet puppet. The Soviets did execute Imré Nagy of Hungary, but not Alexander Dubcek of Czechoslovakia; Dubcek would survive to be chosen to head the nation's democratically elected parliament in 1989.

450. (E) The city of Berlin was many miles inside the Soviet zone of occupation in eastern Germany. In 1948, while Germany was still officially one nation, the Soviets blocked all Allied ground access into the Allied zones of Berlin, claiming that they had the right to do this because the roads, railways, and bridges leading to Berlin were in the Soviet zone of Germany. This created a state of siege; the Allied solution was to fly supplies in over the barricades. The Soviets ended the blockade in 1949, realizing it was not accomplishing their goal.

451. (E) The period immediately following Stalin's death was referred to as "the Thaw," a word that aptly described the slow, cautious process of liberal reform and de-Stalinization that took place beginning with Khrushchev's rise to power. Major peace talks with the United States would take place somewhat later, under Khrushchev's successors; U.S.-Soviet relations during this period would remain hostile. The four reforms described in Choices A through D, however, began within the first year of Khrushchev's administration.

452. (D) World War II effectively ended the many centuries of European domination of the globe. The European powers rebuilt their economies and even thrived in the postwar era, but their era of domination over large far-flung empires was over.

453. (A) Both the nation of Austria and the city of Vienna were occupied by four of the victorious Allied nations immediately after the war. In 1955, the Soviet Union and the United States signed a treaty—the Allied troops of occupation would withdraw from Austria, in exchange for a Soviet guarantee of Austrian neutrality.

454. (A) Choice B represents only the American point of view; Choice C represents the point of view of the Soviets and also of Britain and France. Choices D and E describe fears that may have existed privately in many individual hearts and minds, but that did not constitute matters of serious national concern anywhere. Only Choice A explains why all sides supported the partition of Germany—because its status, whether weak or strong, would largely determine the status of Europe.

455. (B) Nationalism swept through all the formerly European-controlled colonies of Africa and Asia during the Cold War era. (In some areas, such as India, nationalism had been a rising force since before World War II.) Both Vietnamese and Indonesians were determined to expel the foreign authorities and take charge of their own governments. The Netherlands recognized Indonesian independence in December 1949; the French withdrew from Vietnam in 1956, leaving it to sort out its own civil war with the aid of American and Chinese troops. It took a further 20 years until the end of combat and official reunification of North and South Vietnam.

456. (C) Throughout the Cold War, Western Europeans were faced with the fear of Soviet nuclear missiles. The USSR showed no disposition to launch an attack on Western Europe, but the Western European nations were allies of the United States and were pledged to defend it if the Soviets attacked it.

457. (E) Stalin did not believe in genuine alliances between free and independent nations; rather, he believed that a strong nation could only maintain an alliance by forcing control and dominance on a weaker nation. This was the policy he pursued throughout Eastern Europe during and after World War II.

458. (B) Despite its staggering losses of soldiers and civilians during the war, the Soviet Union still had a much larger population than the United States; it was geographically far larger and home to about three times as many people.

459. (B) Poland would remain a one-party Communist state until the rise of Solidarity in the 1980s. The other reforms all took place as described when Gomulka rose to power after Stalin's death, but unfortunately they did not all last and they were not all carried out efficiently. After 1960, censorship tightened once again, the government found itself at odds with the Church again, and the economic reforms did not lead to prosperity.

460. (D) The League of Nations was an international peacekeeping organization established after World War I. NATO is an agreement among the Western nations to come to the defense of any member nation that is attacked. The Quadruple Alliance was the first international peacekeeping organization; it was formed at the end of the Napoleonic Wars. The Warsaw Pact is similar to NATO, but its members were all the Communist nations of Eastern Europe.

461. (A) Before the Berlin Wall was constructed, anyone in East Berlin could simply walk, bicycle, or take the subway into West Berlin and thence to any part of the non-Communist world. Thousands used these simple means to defect—nearly 20 percent of the East German population had fled to the West by 1961.

462. (C) The foreign-policy failures described in Choice A caused the Soviet Union international embarrassment. The overspending in Choice B was a poor investment since the nations the Soviets aided were not reliable allies; additionally, it aroused resentment within the USSR, where most people did not have enough to eat. The vilification, sometimes criminalization, of internationally praised writers such as Boris Pasternak and Joseph Brodsky as described in Choice D made the USSR look bad to the entire world. The agricultural policies described in Choice E included overestimating how much the land could produce, and at the same time underestimating how high the demand would be. De-Stalinization was one area in which Khrushchev accurately read the mood of his fellow Party members and of the nation at large.

463. (B) The Marshall Plan was much more than a charitable handout to provide war-torn Europe with urgent short-term needs such as food and clothing. Its aims were much broader; it was intended to enable Europe to rethink the economic policies that had been in place for centuries. In brief, those who conceived the Marshall Plan believed that the time for individualism in Europe was over; that nations must be encouraged to work together, because this was the only way to maintain peace and prosperity for all. Therefore Choice B, economic self-sufficiency, was the opposite of the Marshall Plan's aims.

464. (C) During the last year of the war, the Italian Resistance took private revenge on thousands of Fascists by executing them. The government attempted to carry out a purge, putting the Fascists on trial in the courts, but there was widespread lack of cooperation, largely because the judges found it too difficult to assess responsibility or agree that crimes had been committed. Someone who had cooperated with the Fascist government was not necessarily a committed Fascist; and cooperating with the government should not be tried as a crime. Faced with widespread distaste for pursuing organized revenge against the Fascists, the government issued a general amnesty in 1946.

465. (C) Adenauer's policy was to ignore the existence of the states behind the Iron Curtain, because they officially recognized East Germany. He himself refused to do so. His view was that there was only one Germany, part of which was occupied by hostile Soviets; he would not recognize the existence of a separate East German state. In fact, the West German constitution prohibited such official recognition.

466. (B) The Supreme Soviet was Russia's legislative body, although it had been nothing but a rubber stamp for the premier since the days of Stalin. Under Gorbachev's reforms, the Supreme Soviet created the Congress of People's Deputies. The CDP comprised 2,250 members as follows: one-third were elected under current rules, representing all the nationalities within the USSR; one-third were elected under current rules, equally representing the people on a geographical basis; and the final third were directly nominated by institutions such as the trade unions and the Soviet youth organization. The CDP members would then elect a new Supreme Soviet that would function as a true parliament.

467. (D) One example of Choice A is the Hungarian revolution led by Imré Nagy in 1956. One example of Choice B is Boris Pasternak's *Doctor Zhivago*, which was in large part responsible for his winning the Nobel Prize in Literature (the USSR forced him to turn down the award). One example of Choice C is Mikhail Baryshnikov, who defected from his native USSR to the West in 1974 and became the greatest international ballet star of the era. One Example of Choice E is the Solidarity movement in Poland.

468. (A) The protest movement that began in Italy around 1968 was never very defined or organized. It consisted of various groups of the population who felt that the government had let them down, but whose goals were often contradictory. For example, the students had a generalized antipathy toward consumerism, but the working classes wanted greater purchasing power with which to buy more material goods. The university system was overcrowded, wages and benefits were lower in Italy than in most of Western Europe, and women were becoming more and more vocal in their demands for rights such as divorce. There were protest movements throughout the West during the 1960s, but Italy's lasted longer and was more militant than most.

469. (A) Dubcek was a committed Socialist who had no intention of abandoning or weakening one-party Communist rule in Czechoslovakia. His view was that rule by force, fear, and repression perverted the ideals of Socialism. He envisioned a democratic brand of Socialism that allowed for freedom of expression, freedom of the press, individual rights to travel and study abroad. He believed that a responsible Communist government need not operate in secret, but should be open and accountable to the citizens for its actions. He supported equality between the Czech and Slovak populations of the country, hoping to restructure the constitution to bring this about. He also set up a commission to investigate the purge trials held by the Soviets during the 1950s, and to achieve justice for those who had wrongly been imprisoned.

470. (B) Czechoslovakia broke apart into two states along ethnic and cultural lines: Slovakia or the Slovak Republic, and the Czech Republic.

471. (D) The bureaucracy is a part of the establishment of any government and therefore is never a revolutionary force. The Catholic Church joined the secular intellectuals in fighting for human rights in Communist Poland. Dock workers and factory workers had staged repeated waves of strikes, finally gaining substantial concessions in 1980. Despite having been under Communist rule since 1945, Poland still had a political opposition, headed after 1976 by a group called the Committee for the Defense of Workers (known by the Polish acronym KOR).

472. (A) The opening of the gates between Eastern and Western Europe was still several years in the future. The other four choices all describe the major goals of the sessions. Thirty-seven participating nations, including the United States and Canada, signed the agreement in Helsinki in 1975.

473. (E) De Gaulle did resign less than a year after the May 1968 events, but they did not factor into his decision except perhaps indirectly, by providing a stressful situation from which he was slow to recover. De Gaulle resigned from a combination of advanced age (he was 79 years old and would die in 1970), the defeat of a referendum whose passage he supported, and sheer personal stubbornness.

474. (C) The post-Stalin era in the Soviet Union is generally referred to as "the Thaw." Repression did not entirely melt away, but the worst excesses of Stalin's regime came to an end. Censorship and other state controls were relaxed as well.

475. (E) *Glasnost* is loosely translated to mean "openness." Gorbachev believed that open discussion of political issues contributed significantly to the strength of the Western states, and he adopted this policy as soon as he took office.

476. (C) The CIS is not analogous to the United States of America, which is a federal republic whose states are self-governing but must obey the same national constitution. Member nations of the CIS are entirely independent and self-governing; they are linked for their mutual benefit only in certain areas of policy.

477. (E) Solidarity began as a trade union but quickly became a major force in Polish politics. The Communist rulers banned it for a time, but were forced to bring it back when it proved too strong for them. Lech Walesa, a leader of Solidarity, eventually became the president of a democratic Poland.

478. (C) By November 1989, popular demonstrations had made it clear to the East Germans that they could not stem the tide of protest for much longer. An October visit by Mikhail Gorbachev, plus the abrupt announcement by the USSR that it would no longer intervene in the affairs of Iron Curtain nations, strengthened the protests. Travel restrictions were eased, and when a reporter at a press conference asked when the new rules would go into effect, a flustered and ill-prepared official answered "Immediately." When this was made public, thousands of Berliners flocked to the Berlin Wall; the guards accepted the situation and let everyone through who was carrying identification. By midnight both East and West Berliners were literally hacking away at the wall with pickaxes.

479. (A) The Baltic republics are the farthest west of the old Soviet republics, and had a long history of independence before they were swallowed up first by Russia and then by the Soviet Union. They consider themselves separate from the rest of the old USSR in various areas—linguistically, culturally, and historically. The Ukraine is now considered only a participating member, and Georgia recently withdrew from the CIS, but both were full members for most of its existence.

480. (B) France and Germany had been at odds for centuries; ironically, they share a common ethnic and cultural origin in the Frankish tribes of early medieval Europe. This shared heritage was recognized after World War II with the formation of the EEC, which later became known as the European Union.

481. (A) Communists had seized power in Afghanistan in 1978 in the teeth of popular opposition. The Soviets sent troops in 1979, siding with the Communist government in the civil war that followed. The long drawn-out war was enormously costly to the USSR in terms of financial resources and casualties, and brought no political gains. The last Soviet troops withdrew from Afghanistan in 1989.

482. (B) *Perestroika* refers to the restructuring of the government and society, largely by such measures as rolling back censorship, encouraging free speech, and making foreign policy friendlier and more liberal. Choice A defines the term *détente*, and Choice C defines the term *glasnost*.

483. (B) At Solidarity's national congress of 1981, members did vote in favor of an appeal to their fellow workers in all nations behind the Iron Curtain. However, the vote was largely symbolic. In the first place, it was a call for aid rather than an attempt to form an international union; in the second place, no international version of Solidarity developed from it. The other four choices accurately describe Lech Walesa's career as one of Poland's great leaders.

484. (D) Yugoslavia, like the Austrian Empire, was made of too many nationalities that wanted self-determination. Eventually it broke apart into a number of small states.

485. (C) Protest in the USSR during the 1960s had concentrated on the circulation of forbidden books—a phenomenon called *samizdat* in Russian. In the 1970s, *samizdat* was no longer a largely literary phenomenon; it had expanded to include political pamphlets, books, and essays, many from Yugoslavia and Czechoslovakia. The movement grew by tens of thousands of new members, including whole segments of Soviet society who had been outside it before, such as political prisoners and ethnic minorities. The establishment of the Human Rights Committee in 1970 gave the dissident movement a formal central organization. However, it did not at this time succeed in persuading or forcing much change of national policy.

486. (A) The government was afraid of the possible consequences of reintroducing martial law in response to the strikes and demonstrations, therefore it did not attempt it. Instead, the government's leaders invited the leaders of the opposition to sit down with them and try together to resolve the severe economic and labor crisis.

487. **(E)** Franco had promised that after his death or retirement, he would restore the monarchy. Most Spaniards greeted this oft-repeated promise with skepticism, but in fact Franco named Prince Juan Carlos as his successor. Since Juan Carlos's father was still living and was thus the legitimate king, this angered some people. In the end, Juan Carlos's father formally renounced any claim to the throne, and Spain's transition to rule by a freely elected Cortés with a constitutional monarch was surprisingly swift and peaceful.

488. **(B)** *Ostpolitik* means "Eastern policy." Brandt's thinking was somewhat ahead of his time, and was received with suspicion in the East and disapproval in the West. He stopped short of official diplomatic recognition of East Germany (which was banned in the West German constitution), but he did make it clear that he accepted the existence of the divided state and that he wished for friendly relations between the two sides. His interest in holding talks with Czech and Polish leaders showed that he was ready to accept the postwar borders of these states—a position that aroused hostility in the West.

489. **(A)** Thatcher's stubborn adherence to a platform of conservative economic policies that represented a radical break from Britain's recent political past resulted in a dismal economic climate, described in Choices B through D. Historians agree that she would have been swiftly voted out of office had it not been for Britain's efficient handling of the Falklands War in 1982. However, Thatcher could point to success in some areas. Britain's gross domestic product grew at about the same pace as the rest of Europe, individual incomes rose, and several previously nationalized industries were privatized.

490. **(C)** Jaruzelski's appointment was a signal that the Polish government was preparing to crack down on the signs of opposition that had proved such a potent force for reform in Poland, especially the formation of Solidarity as a national trade union that soon developed into a major political party. The election of a Polish pope and the awarding of the Nobel Prize in Literature to a Polish writer brought the nation into international prominence in 1980; with all eyes on Poland, the government hesitated to provoke the people to any further displays of opposition.

491. **(E)** The Helsinki agreement of 1975 gave rise to Charter 77, a dissident movement that issued a document claiming that the Czechoslovakian government routinely violated its own laws. The signers of Charter 77 pointed out that Czechoslovakia had signed a number of international treaties (including the Helsinki agreement) that explicitly affirmed such rights as freedom of the press, freedom of expression, the workers' right to establish trade unions, and the right to privacy. Therefore, government repression in any of these areas meant that Czechoslovakia was in violation of these treaties. Charter 77 had little effect on the Czech government; it was a small movement, and its leaders were summarily tried and imprisoned. However, Charter 77 did win widespread international support and thus helped to change the climate of repression behind the Iron Curtain.

492. (A) Choice A helps to explain why the United States pursued *détente*; U.S. president Nixon wanted Soviet support for a peace settlement, not the other way around. The other four choices outline the major factors in Brezhnev's willingness to sit down with Nixon at the conference table. China had become a Communist giant since World War II, and its relationship to the USSR had grown steadily more inimical. Faced with major threats from both China and the United States, the USSR opted to try to come to a better understanding with the United States. Brezhnev also hoped that easing trade barriers would benefit the Soviet economy.

493. (A) The workers' arguments for higher wages and greater benefits were justified, given that Italians were worse off in this regard than most other Western Europeans. The government was willing to make economic concessions that pacified the workers and thus helped to destroy any threat of social revolution. Regional government had been constitutionally guaranteed before 1950, but had been slow to materialize. The divorce law was fiercely argued on both sides of the government, but was overwhelmingly popular among the citizens.

494. (B) May 1968 saw a major national uprising that included student protests and national workers' strikes. There were calls for social and political revolution, the loosening of the tight government control over television and the press, and higher wages. Owing to effective opposition from the government, the police, and even the Communist Party, the May 1968 movement ended almost before it began; it was disorganized, inefficient, and divided in its goals.

495. (D) Tito was in the forefront of the fighting when Yugoslavia was liberated during World War II. Quickly rising to political prominence, he oversaw the creation of a mixed economy with elements of both Socialism and capitalism. Under Tito's leadership, Yugoslavians enjoyed many basic privileges denied to other nationalities behind the Iron Curtain. Tito was the only Communist leader to defy all Soviet attempts to interfere with him; he insisted on maintaining Yugoslavia's independent sovereignty, and refused to take sides throughout the Cold War. Tito received many international honors during his lifetime, but was never awarded the Nobel Prize.

496. (E) Franco was a highly pragmatic ruler, keeping a sharp eye on the mood of his subjects and constantly shifting the rules and policies of his government to meet current needs. The passage of the new constitution and the laws described in Choices A through D to implement that constitution marked the beginnings of Spain's eventual transition toward a freer and more democratic society.

497. (B) In 1989, an overwhelming tide of popular anti-Communist sentiment throughout the nation made Communist leader Gustav Husak decide to resign. Within the month, Vaclav Havel was chosen as the new president in a democratic election. At the same time, Alexander Dubcek became the new head of the Czechoslovakian parliament.

498. (C) The spectacular rise of Solidarity and the government's concessions to it alarmed the Soviets, who applied steady pressure on newly elected Prime Minister Jaruzelski to crack down on the rebels. A Soviet invasion to restore order was a very real possibility. Jaruzelski also feared the possibilities of civil war and a total economic collapse, given that the workers' movement was proving so strong and had such a vast popular following. He declared martial law only a few days before an announced Solidarity demonstration in Warsaw that might well have overturned the government. The one thing that was not a factor in his decision was Choice C; no free elections had been announced.

499. (E) The largest and most powerful among the Communist nations and the instigator of the Cold War was, fittingly, the last nation to give up on Communism. The Soviet Union was officially dissolved as of December 31, 1991.

500. (A) The Soviet Union famously trumped the United States in a "space race" between the two superpowers when Soviet astronaut Yuri Gagarin became the first human being to orbit the Earth. This was in the early 1960s, long before Gorbachev's rise to power.